Ways of Thinking, Ways of Teaching

Ways of Thinking, Ways of Teaching

George Hillocks, Jr.

FOREWORD BY LEE SHULMAN

Teacher College, Columbia University
New York and London

Published by Teachers College Press, 1234 Amsterdam Avenue, New York, NY 10027

Library of Congress Cataloging-in-Publication Data

Hillocks, George.
     Ways of thinking, ways of teaching / George Hillocks, Jr. :
   foreword by Lee Shulman.
          p.   cm.
     Includes bibliographical references and index.
     ISBN 0-8077-3804-2 (cloth: acid-free paper).—ISBN 0-8077-3803-4 (pbk.
 : acid-free paper)
     1. English language—Rhetoric—Study and teaching.   2. Community
college teachers—United States—Interviews.   3. English teachers—
United States—Interviews.   I. Shulman, Lee.   II. Title.
PE1408.H5719   1998
428'.007'173—DC21   98-37044

ISBN 0-8077-3803-4 (paper)
ISBN 0-8077-3804-2 (cloth)

Printed on acid-free paper
Manufactured in the United States of America

06 05 04 03 02 01 00 99   8 7 6 5 4 3 2 1

Contents

Foreword by Lee Shulman   vii
Acknowledgments   xi

1   Matters of Significance: Differences Among Teachers   1

What Teachers Know   2
What Knowledge Is Essential for Teaching   5
Unpacking Assumptions   17
The Plan of the Present Study   20

2   Knowledge in Classrooms   22

Knowledge in Performance   23
Knowledge in Classrooms   24
Analyzing Knowledge in Observed Classrooms   29

3   Profiles of Teaching   38

What Proportion of Time Is Spent on Instruction?   38
What Kinds of Activities Characterize
   the Delivery of Knowledge?   39
What Is the Nature and Variation of Knowledge Taught?   39
What Factors May Account for Differences Among Teachers?   41
Teacher Attitudes and Beliefs About Students   43
Explanations and Summary of Categorizations   46
Teaching and Attitudes Toward Students   48
Attitude and Type of Knowledge   49
Attitude and Mode of Knowledge   50

4   Knowledge of Students, Purpose, and Content   53

Teaching Formal Discourse Knowledge   53
Feedback on Writing   65
Categories of Teacher Knowledge   69
Some Dynamics of Teacher Knowledge   72

5   Substance and Constructivist Teaching   75

    Substantive Knowledge   75
    The Heart of the Difference   91

6   The Construction of Curriculum   94

    Professor Dobbs   95
    Professor Kramer   101
    Curriculum Knowledge and the Development of Curriculum   105

7   The Dynamics of Teacher Thinking   109

    Epistemological Stance and Rhetoric   109
    Practical Learning Theory   113
    Curriculum and Goals   115
    Epistemological Stance and Curriculum   117
    Conceptions of Students and Curriculum   119
    Pedagogical Content Knowledge   120
    Conclusions About Teacher Thinking   123
    Teacher Knowledge and Identity   124

8   Implications   126

    Teacher Change and Reflective Practice   126
    Implications for Teacher Change   134
    Implications for Research   137

References   139
Index   143
About the Author   149

Foreword

YOU ARE ABOUT TO READ George Hillocks's exquisite account of the thinking, pedagogical practices, and reflections of a fascinating group of English teachers. No two are quite alike. They range from rather conservative to daringly radical in their views of both their discipline and the likelihood that their students will succeed. The differences among them are respectfully delineated and examined. Hillocks wishes us to appreciate the extent to which, while ostensibly teaching the same subject, their practice grows from quite different understandings of the nature of writing, of literature, and of learning to write and read well. And, argues Hillocks, initiatives to reform our schools will surely founder if they ignore the centrality of those teacher conceptions, beliefs, and practices. Educational change must always be mediated through the minds and motives of teachers.

Far too much of the rhetoric of school reform orignates from impossibly simple conceptions of schooling. Some reformers place their bets heavily on the development of new national and state standards. Make standards explicit (and tough!), develop thorough examinations for holding students (and teachers) accountable to those standards, and conditions will improve. They are probably correct.

Other reformers identify aspects of the organization of schooling, such as class or school size. Reduce class sizes to a maximum of 22 in the primary grades, offered the governor of California. Shift from large, comprehensive urban high schools to smaller, more intimate schools that can function as face-to-face communities, claim Deborah Meier and many others. As I read their arguments, I am sure that both smaller classes and smaller schools contribute significantly to improved education.

Still others point at the teachers as the key to reform, arguing that too many teachers simply don't understand enough subject matter to guide their students to the promised land of higher achievement. These critics, such as Boston University's John Silber, would raise the bar for *teachers'* test scores, GPAs, and other indicators of their intellectual and subject-matter rigor. And they are probably right, as well.

I am reminded at these times of the classic story of the Rabbi of Chelm, the mythical town of fools, before whom appeared two men, each claiming ownership of the same chicken. When the first man finished offering his argument, the rabbi nodded vigorously and exclaimed, "You're right, the chicken is clearly yours." Then the second man presented the basis for his claim, after which the rabbi again nodded vigorously and asserted, "No question, the chicken is yours." As the men stood before the rabbi trying to parse these two conclusions, the rabbi's wife, who had been observing the proceedings, leaned over and whispered to her somewhat addled spouse, "But, my dear, they can't *both* be right!" The rabbi stroked his long beard, gazed admiringly at his wise wife, and assented, "You know, you're also right!"

Complex systems, such as classrooms and schools, cannot depend on simple single-cause models to guide their improvement or reform. While it is typically impossible to disagree with the prescriptions (higher standards, smaller schools, smarter teachers, rigorous curriculum, etc.), reforms that treat each of these in isolation appear doomed to futility. So how does George Hillocks propose to improve the situation? By first making it even more complicated.

Most leaders in the worlds of policy and practice implore their siblings in scholarship to make their work more simple so that it can be applied more readily. One of the reasons why I find so much to admire in George Hillocks's work is that he recognizes that we must understand a phenomenon's complexity before we can simplify it in the interests of policy. This is a book that examines the work of a number of teachers of English and writing and asks about the major influences on their pedagogy. In particular, Hillocks asks a set of questions about their understanding—of their discipline, of their students, of their own ongoing learning as teachers—and about how their thinking affects their teaching. Moreover, he goes beyond the simplistic view that would attribute teaching excellence to the *amount* of knowledge the teachers hold about their subject. He asks, instead, how the *ways they make sense* of their subject, their conceptions of what counts as knowledge in English, and their conceptions of their students' capacities to acquire that knowledge influence their own attempts to make their subject clear, comprehensible, compelling, and consequential for their students.

Hillocks places special emphasis on two aspects of the teachers' thinking: their epistemological beliefs about what constitutes significant knowledge in their field, and their deeply held beliefs about the likelihood that their students will be successful in learning to understand what they teach. Although his categories are more conceptually rich than I portray here, he basically claims that there are two kinds of epistemological belief systems: objectivist and constructivist. Teachers either believe that the knowledge is "out there" to be apprehended and internalized, or that it only becomes knowledge when the "buzzing, blooming confusion" out there is constructed actively into knowledge by the learner. With respect to expectations for their students, teachers are either optimists or pessimists. Thus, we can have *objectivist pessimists* (the knowledge is out there waiting to be learned, but the students are just not smart enough to get it), *constructivist optimists* (the knowledge is theirs to construct, and by golly, they are going to do it), *objectivist optimists*, and *constructivist pessimists*. For some reason, that last category has no empirical instances in this study. Perhaps you can't survive as a constructivist if you are not simultaneously deeply optimistic.

Most teachers in Hillocks's study fall into the *objectivist pessimist* category, and that is not good news for reformers. Moreover, during the two years of the research, it was quite rare to find someone changing orientations. That is, most of the postsecondary teachers of English whom Hillocks studied came to their pedagogical responsibilities with an epistemic sense of their subject as relatively fixed and given. They viewed their students' capacities for learning the subject as rather fixed as well. And they showed little inclination to modify those beliefs over time.

While Hillocks expresses pessimism about the capacity of veteran teachers to change their beliefs, and hence their practices, he expresses some hope that if one could begin the socialization of teachers during their preparation period, more change might occur. Our own reasearch suggests that he is correct. Novice teachers are more likely to enter the profession with much more optimistic (some might say idealistic) expectations for their students, and the often constructivist orientations of teacher education programs help to support those beliefs. But what can be done about the beliefs of teachers in the community colleges (such as those studied in this book) and the rest of postsecondary education, who ordinarily have no pedagogical preparation whatsoever? This is a challenge that we at the Carnegie Foundation for the Advancement of Teaching are addressing in several of our ongoing projects.

Hillocks also makes the compelling argument that one's scholarly conception of a subject carries with it an inherent conception of its pedagogy, and warns against the inclination to separate content from pedagogy, or to distinguish the scholarly understanding of a subject from its pedagogical understanding. He emphasizes the centrality of the teacher's role in transforming his or her understanding of the subject for pedagogical purposes, and attributes much of that capacity to transform to the character of the disciplinary conceptions.

I suspect that the usefulness of such distinctions depends heavily on differences among subject matters, and even within them. Perhaps it is much harder to think about the difference between knowing writing and teaching writing than it is to contemplate the distinction between knowing mathematics and teaching mathematics. And even within English, there are certainly differences between grammar and literary analysis. There may well be differences between novice teachers, who hold those areas more separately, and veterans, who have integrated them. There may also be differences between postsecondary teachers, who have rarely had the benefit of specific pedagogical preparation, and K–12 teachers, who have studied pedagogy more explicitly.

If I am critical of any aspect of this book, it is a criticism that I level at most of my own work as well. Hillocks takes a decidedly psychological approach to the problem of teacher knowledge and teaching practice. He entertains the possibility that context plays a role in the shaping and sustaining of those beliefs and practices, and dismisses the hypothesis rather quickly. I think that in this matter, he and I have both erred. The work of Milbrey McLaughlin and Joan Talbert of Stanford has confirmed repeatedly that variations among secondary-school departments in the teaching practices of their faculty members can be attributed significantly to context-driven differences in their beliefs about both their subjects and their students. Moreover, Susan Stodolsky and Pamela Grossman have demonstrated how department-based variations in teachers' epistemic beliefs and beliefs about students influence their openness to reform initiatives. Since Grossman and Stodolsky have contrasted English and mathematics departments, their work should be read in conjunction with that of Hillocks. It may well be that changing the context in which one teaches can have more influence on beliefs and practices than any individual interventions can hope to accomplish.

This fine work is a model for many important values in educational scholarship. It demonstrates how meticulously evidence can be gathered and displayed to analyze a complex set of relationships between knowledge and teaching. George Hillocks is above all a superb methodologist. The book takes theory very seriously, and weaves theoretical work together with empirical findings. It exemplifies how inquiries that bridge subject matter, psychological theory, and pedagogical practice are nurtured in a superb department of education by a scholar who holds full citizenship in both the liberal arts and the profession of education. It thus makes us even sadder to observe that the fine University of Chicago department in which George Hillocks has flourished will soon be but a memory.

Enjoy this book and learn from it. You will profit from the experience.

Lee Shulman
Carnegie Foundation for the Advancement of Teaching

Acknowledgments

THIS BOOK WOULD NOT have been possible without the generous grant from the Ford Foundation that made my work with community college professors possible. The Ford grant allowed for the collection of data and a great deal of the analysis. A grant from the Research Foundation of the National Council of Teachers of English helped in the detailed analysis of certain cases. I am greatly indebted to both.

Many people contributed to the collection of the data and their primary and secondary analysis. Tom Albritton served as the project manager and scheduled and smoothed the way for interviews and classroom observations and made many of them himself. Charles Rogers worked on collecting data and keeping the massive amounts of material in order. Over the two years of data collection, Robert Cosgrove, Jo Hillocks, George Snyder, John Whitehurst, and Sharon Rollow observed classes and conducted interviews after classes. This was a very tough job. Perhaps the most difficult work of all was the first level of analysis, which involved listening to recordings of classrooms, reading transcripts and observer notes, and coding the classroom events minute by minute, using a very complex coding system. Had I known what I do now, I would have made that job simpler from the start. But I did not, and I am grateful to Ellen Anderson, David Anderson, Dennis Murawski, Jo Hillocks, and Sally Harrold for their efforts. A second team rechecked the codings and timings, mainly to ensure that the categorization of various events as diversions was appropriate and accurate. For this, I am grateful to Brian Fischer, Risa Gottlieb, Jamie Kowalczyk, Kevin Perks, and Jeremy Perney for their efficient and hard work.

Several graduate students worked on the interpretation of individual cases when the data seemed to be an uncharted sea. I am grateful to Seok Hong, Sherri Koeppen, Steve Littell, and Liz Miller for their work in this regard. The anonymous reviewers for Teachers College Press were both helpful and supportive in commenting on my first submission to the Press. When I came to the full manuscript stage, I benefited from the good advice of Kendra Sisserson and Bruce Novak. Finally, I have had excellent advice from Carol Chambers Collins and meticulous editing from Lyn Grossman, both of Teachers College Press. All of these people have done their best to save me from my own blunders. I can only hope they have succeeded.

Ways of Thinking, Ways of Teaching

Matters of Significance:
Differences Among Teachers

IF WE WERE TO VISIT the teachers who will be the subject of this study, we would see vastly different approaches to teaching English 100. We would see one teacher focus on specially devised exercises to teach mechanical correctness, another dictate passages that students duly write out, and which are punctuated in different ways on different days so that the students will attend to the sounds of speech and their corresponding representations in writing, and a third ask students to read model paragraphs and proceed through a variety of steps to promote the writing of such brief paragraphs. A fourth teacher of English 100 focuses on personal narrative writing and requires that his students produce 80 pages over the semester, generating ideas for writing in class through seeing and recalling images from passages read and from experiences remembered. The differences among these approaches to teaching are enormous, and they promote similar disparities in the experiences of students in the classes. Connelly and Clandinin (1988) claim that all "matters of significance" in classrooms are the result of what they call teachers' personal knowledge. That may be the case. Certainly, differences in knowledge or conceptions of teaching must be associated with such differences.

In the first book of the *Metaphysics*, Aristotle argues that the main difference between master craftsmen and manual workers lies in the former's grasp of the theory underlying what they do. They have learned their art through study and not simply through repeated experience. They understand the reasons for doing what they do, which leads him to write:

> In general it is a sign of the man who knows and the man who does not know, that the former can teach and . . . men of mere experience cannot. (Aristotle, 1947, p. 244)

Unfortunately, Aristotle does not go on explicate what master craftsmen possess in addition to a grasp of theory and an understanding of the reasons for acting as they do: what, if any, knowledge they may have that enables them to move beyond performing their arts to teaching. Is it enough to know the reasons for doing what an art requires, the underlying theory, or is there some knowledge that is peculiar to teaching it? Is there a body of knowledge that underlies the art of teaching itself? If so, how do those who teach conceptualize it? If the preceding examples are any indication, can we talk about such a body of knowledge in the singular?

Such questions have been the focus of burgeoning research on teacher thinking. Fenstermacher (1994), in his review of the epistemological dimensions of research on teacher thinking, provides an overview of the literature on "teacher knowledge," organizing the issues under four questions, two of which are of concern in this book:

1. What do teachers know?
2. What knowledge is essential for teaching?

For the first question, Fenstermacher considers two lines of research. One develops from the work of Clandinin and Connelly focusing on personal practical knowledge of teaching and the ways that teachers encapsulate it. The other line develops out of the work of Schön (1987) and his ideas about reflective practice. (Because of its dependency on other aspects of teacher knowledge, I will consider Schön's work in a later chapter.) Fenstermacher gives Shulman (1986, 1987) and his students (e.g., Grossman, 1990) credit for instigating research related to the second question: What knowledge is essential for teaching?

WHAT TEACHERS KNOW

The work of Elbaz (1983) and that of Clandinin and Connelly have been an effort to determine what teachers know that others do not and how teachers encapsulate that knowledge. That is to say, many people may know the content of what teachers attempt to teach. However, teachers also have knowledge about teaching that simply sharing the content knowledge does not provide. The ideas of these researchers are based on classroom observation and the analysis of what teachers say about their work. Elbaz (1983) studied one high school teacher, Clandinin (1986) studied two teachers at the kindergarten and first-grade level, and together Clandinin and Connelly (1995) have studied teachers in schools for a much longer period.

Their goal has been to examine teachers' "personal practical knowledge," a term used, according to Connelly and Clandinin (1988), "to emphasize the teacher's knowing of a classroom" (p. 25). The idea underlying the term, they say, is comparable to Elbaz's (1983) concept of *practical knowledge*. They say that "it is teachers' 'personal knowledge' that determines all matters of significance relative to the planned conduct of classrooms. So 'personal knowledge' is the key term" (p. 4).

Connelly and Clandinin (1988) say that "personal practical knowledge . . . is a particular way of reconstructing the past and the intentions for the future to deal with the exigencies of a present situation" (p. 25). This personal knowledge resides in "the person's past experience, in the person's present mind and body, and in the person's future plans and actions" (p. 25) and is represented in life narratives that are composed of many short stories characterized by Connelly and Clandinin as being subjective and having a "rich affective quality" because they are the result of lived experiences. The affective quality of the stories and narratives means that they are unavoidably imbued with values and aesthetics. As Connelly and Clandinin (1988) put it:

> [O]ur experiences, and therefore our personal practical knowledge that makes up our narratives, are never devoid of these affective matters. To know something is to feel something. To know something is to value something. To know something is to respond aesthetically. (p. 26)

Following Elbaz (1983), Connelly and Clandinin (1988) add that personal practical knowledge is encapsulated in other ways: in images, rules, practical principles, personal philosophy, metaphor, narrative unity, and rhythm. By *image* they mean "something within our experience, embodied in us as persons and expressed and enacted in our practices and actions." Stephanie, one of the two teachers in Clandinin (1986), for example, talks about her classroom as a "home" and about "planting seeds" to see if students will be interested in an activity. Such images, according to Connelly and Clandinin, help drive the kinds of activities and attitudes that appear in her classroom.

Another term that Connelly and Clandinin (1988) use is *metaphor*. Their talk about it is similar to their talk about image. They say, "We view metaphors as important parts of our personal practical knowledge and as a central form in our language of practice. We understand teachers' actions and practices as embodied expressions of their metaphors of teaching and of living" (p. 71). As with images, metaphors are "derived from our personal, historical, and cultural narratives." They "structure the way we act in the present and guide our future practices" (p. 70).

Agreeing with Elbaz (1983), Connelly and Clandinin (1988) define *rules* as briefly formulated statements about what to do in specific situations. *Practical principles* are simply less specific formulations that also include statements of the teacher's purposes and are applicable in a fairly wide variety of situations. Although Connelly and Clandinin claim that "the statement of a principle contains a rationale that emerges at the end of a process of deliberation on a problem," they do not provide an instance of that process. Both rules and principles appear as more or less disembodied claims about teaching policy.

Personal philosophy names the way a teacher thinks about him- or herself in teaching situations, but stated in narrative form. That is, although the personal philosophy involves values and beliefs, the values and rules are not stated directly. Rather, "they are submerged within the narrative that contains the personal, situational meaning of events." Connelly and Clandinin (1988) "mean much more than just an 'explanation' and/or statement of what we believe" (p. 67). In an illustrative example, a researcher asks why a teacher, Bruce, when teaching his science class, had his students copy notes, apparently from a handout, a pattern of note taking different from that in this teacher's geography and history units. At first Bruce comments that the note taking is to prepare students for ninth-grade science, "where they'll have to do large copious notes." The researcher is interested in why the students copied the notes from a handout rather than making their own notes. To get at this, the researcher explains what he had observed on various occasions:

> SIAKA: Let me go over what I have observed (sure). Sometimes you dictated notes (oh yeah, yeah) that the students had to copy. Sometimes they received handouts that they copied, (right) sometimes they read with you. . . . You went through questions that they then wrote the answers to.
>
> BRUCE: Alright. Got it. You're still talking about science. The reasons I would go with copying notes is I was running out of time and I wanted them to have a note. And if they do an individual note it means that I will have to look them over. I did not have time. We didn't have the time to look at 28 individual notes. Therefore it was a matter of convenience that we did the same notes together. Just like me dictating. We need 14 months during the school year. We can't do it. So that was the whole reason behind that. (p. 67)

Connelly and Clandinin (1988) comment that "Bruce does not talk about the nature of science nor about what his purposes were. . . . Our first hint as to how Bruce thinks about science teaching, then, is that it reflects his own energies and capabilities, on the one hand, and, on the other, the overall program he intends to offer for the Grade 7 year" (p. 68). That is, Bruce's decision to have students copy notes results from his ideas about the goals of the present course (to prepare students in note taking) and concern for his own time and energy.

I am not sure how such thinking qualifies as philosophy, personal or otherwise. What Connelly and Clandinin (1988) identify as personal philosophy seem to me to be more like personal guidelines for decision making. Certainly, teachers make use of such guidelines, and they are important to consider. Underlying Bruce's guidelines are certain conceptions of teaching, learning, and epistemology. For example, Bruce assumes, first, that taking notes is important to learning; second, that copying a ready-made note will have the same effect on learning as will constructing a note; and third, that if students copy a note, they can be assumed to copy it in the same way, thereby eliminating the need for him to check the notes. However, Connelly and Clandinin do not comment on these or other assumptions.

Nevertheless, I find this a very appealing conceptualization of a certain kind of teacher knowledge. After my 40 years of teaching and working with teachers at middle school, high school, and college levels, much of what Connelly and Clandinin say about teacher thinking rings true for me. When I look back on all those years, I know that I have constructed stories upon stories about my students and our relationships, some funny, warm, and joyous and some that I cannot tell without a conscious effort to hold back tears. All teachers have such stories and images. Mine certainly originate in my past, but they remain very vivid many years later, and, with Connelly and Clandinin (1988), I can say that they "structure the way [I] act in the present and guide [my] future practices" (p. 70).

However, do stories, images, metaphors, rules, principles, and so forth constitute all of teacher knowledge? Can it be true, as Connelly and Clandinin (1988) claim, that "teachers' 'personal knowledge' . . . determines all matters of significance relative to the planned conduct of classrooms" (p. 4)? Elbaz (1991) appears to agree. She claims that

> the story is the very stuff of teaching, the landscape within which we live as teachers and researchers, and within which the work of teachers can be seen as making sense. . . . [This is] an epistemological claim that teachers' knowledge in its own terms is ordered by story and can best be understood in this way. (p. 3)

Interestingly, the stories referred to by these researchers contain virtually no information about the nature of curricula or about the knowledge taught or its conception and construction. These researchers apparently assume that the curriculum is foreordained and that teachers operate *within* its structure; they do not consider how they operate *on* its structure. When a teacher says that he or she is interested in "planting seeds," the researchers do not ask what kind of seeds or the reasons underlying this choice, or how those seeds are to be planted, but are simply concerned with the use of the metaphor. They are not concerned with the content of the note and its presumed purposes in learning, but only with the fact of copying a note. The result is that the research and conceptualization cannot explain the difference between copying a teacher note and developing notes based on a peer-group discussion. Nor can they explain the difference between planting seeds through lecture or through some student-centered activity. I believe that we need such explanations to understand teacher knowledge.

WHAT KNOWLEDGE IS ESSENTIAL FOR TEACHING

Another line of research has had to do with the second question: What knowledge is essential for teaching? Shulman (1986, 1987) outlines a set of categories that have to do with more than personal knowledge related to teaching. His categories have to do with content knowledge, pedagogical content knowledge, and other categories of knowledge that make it possible for teachers to teach particular subjects. Referring to the research on teaching as a generic activity, Shulman (1986) points out that "investigators ignored one central aspect of classroom life: the subject matter" (p. 6). He goes on to comment on the result of this simplification:

> Policy makers . . . find [research on teaching] replete with references to direct instruction, time on task, wait time, ordered turns, lower-order questions, and the like. They find little or no references to subject matter, so the resulting standards or mandates lack any reference to content dimensions of teaching. . . . Even those who studied teacher cognition, a decidedly non-process-product perspective, investigated teacher planning or interactive decision making with little concern for the organization of content knowledge in the minds of teachers. (p. 6)

In this seminal article (1986) and a later one (1987), Shulman proceeds to lay out a hypothetical knowledge base for teaching that includes both generic and subject matter–specific concepts:

1. Knowledge of the subject to be taught
2. General pedagogical knowledge—"those broad principles and strategies of classroom management and organization that appear to transcend subject matter
3. Curriculum knowledge of "materials and programs"
4. "Pedagogical content knowledge, that special amalgam of content and pedagogy that is uniquely the province of teachers"
5. Knowledge of students
6. "Knowledge of educational contexts"
7. "Knowledge of educational ends, purposes, and values" (all quotations from Shulman, 1987, p. 8)

Several studies suggest that these categories are reasonable and useful.

However, even casual observers will note that teachers of the same subject matter may teach in quite different ways with quite different effects. When confronted with such differences, teachers often say simply that there are many paths to the same goal and that they have simply adopted what is most congenial to them. A simple congeniality of "pedagogical content knowledge" or some other category hardly seems to account for the wide differences among teachers of the same subject classes. I suspect that great differences in teaching may amount to differences in ways of thinking about the nature of knowledge, in epistemology. For illustration of these differences, let us turn to two specific cases, bearing in mind two questions: What are the teachers attempting to teach? and, How do they expect students to learn it?

Case 1

In the first example, Professor Wade, a highly experienced community college teacher, begins his freshman composition class with a reminder that "your how-do-you-do-it papers . . . are due this week." After a few other business reminders, he comments, "If you finished those papers, you should be well into thinking about your next paper. I asked you today to come in with a brief explanation of what you're writing about. . . . The classification and division paper, which, as I point out in this criteria here (pointing to a handout), explains an idea by breaking it down into its components, or by showing the varieties of the subject, whatever subject it is you choose."

He goes on to explain that in the previous class session, to show students how "classification or division" applies to "our everyday lives," he had asked students "to list what qualities you think are important in a potential mate" and what qualities the opposite sex thought were important. For the next 6 minutes, the professor lectures on the findings of his survey for three classes that participated. The following excerpt provides the flavor of this lecture:

> I compiled the results which are quite interesting, and I don't want to dwell on it. This is not a sociology class, but if you choose to write about this you may find these results to be interesting. First of all, many more females in my three classes than males. What females want in a man: according to my scoring system the most important thing is honesty, however defined that is. And I will not presume to talk about what honesty is. The second thing was loyalty. Job, money, career, something like that. There were some things that weren't expressed exactly that way. Third most important was appearance, and by that I included everything from smells good to hair cut right to whenever someone said that they decided what was important and listed it in the top five categories that had something to do with the externals. Muscles. Dresses nice. So that's a big category, I realize, and that may be why it scored higher than some of you think it might. The last one was love and caring. Close to understanding and close to maturity. A big problem here of course is we don't know what other people mean by these things.
>
> Now this is what males think women want. Males put more importance on appearance, they think that women really want someone who appears [good]. More men rated that higher than women do. Although it's still pretty high among the women.

During this lecture, which continues for many more lines of transcript, the only student lines are, "I came in a little late. What were we supposed to be doing with this?"

After a brief explanation, the professor turns to what he calls the "telephone pests piece," a composition that had been written by a woman in his class the previous year. He says to his students, "We'll read it together and we'll tear it apart. As we read it make little notes and comments so you can contribute to our discussion of this. Also let's try to assign it point totals, grade it, if you will. And we'll talk about why you're grading it the way you did. Carol do you want to start reading this?" When Carol finishes reading, two other students read about a third each to the end of the essay, taking about 8 minutes of class time. With the reading complete, the professor asks, "Any problems, questions of understanding here? Is it clear to you? Any words? There were some mistakes?" The next 4 minutes are taken up with the professor and three students pointing out various errors and "typos."

Then rather abruptly, the professor changes the focus of attention from mechanics to what he refers to as the structure of the piece:

> What I'd like you to do before we talk about this any further is attempt to . . . see its structure. You'll be using the chicken foot outline that I have presented to you that you're familiar with. It may take another claw, I don't know. Write what you think the thesis or the main idea of this is. Is there a main idea here? Remember, it's often not stated as such. You may have to write down the main idea that you got out of it based on what words were [repeated]. But then again it may be stated, it may be explicit as well as hinted at. What are the categories that this writer breaks the subject down into? And in what order? Does she make that kind of a rough outline? See the structure in it, because you're going to need to make an outline for your own piece. If it looks something like what you'd come up with if you'd looked as carefully. Write it out on a sheet of paper. I'll come around and see if you're having any problems with it.

The reference to the "chicken foot outline" is to a previous class in which Professor Wade drew a straight horizontal line on the board with three or four lines fanning out at the right end to look like a chicken foot, the idea being that the claws grow from the leg, providing a more organic metaphor than the usual explanation of the conventional outline. Professor Wade reminds the students that he is "using this as an example of a classification paper." He then walks around the room, looking down at individual papers to see what students are writing, stopping to speak occasionally with individuals.

PROFESSOR WADE: We'll talk about how you grade it. First see its structure. Show me you see its structure.
IRENE: Show you?

> PROFESSOR WADE: Show the structure of the piece, the outline. You're familiar with the chicken foot, right? (becomes inaudible) Show me that you see a structure here and can explain it to me.

After 9 minutes of students' working at this, the teacher begins a brief question-and-answer period about what they have found: "What is the subject?" (Telephone pests.) "What are the types of telephone pests? What are they? In the order that she presents them." After students identify the various telephone pests, he says,

> You see that listing in the last sentence of the paragraph? That signals how the piece will be structured. And if you look in each paragraph after that, till you get to the concluding two paragraphs, you'll see she follows that structure. The only problem is what is an obnoxious, who are the obnoxious ones? Look at the paragraph about the obnoxious caller.

After explicating the problem of the "obnoxious" category, Professor Wade explains what he was looking for:

> So what I was looking for from you and what appears to be to me the major outline of the piece, the thesis would be being an operator is not easy because of the types of telephone pests there are. One type was the obnoxious, one type was the rude, one type was the impatient, another type was the pervert. . . . One could do worse than to follow this particular scheme. Now there are some problems with it.

Then, Professor Wade conducts a 20-minute discussion of the problems (until the class ends), in which he asks questions about problems in the essay, explicates their nature, and explains how to repair them. Of 228 transcript lines of talk for this section, he has spoken 164, or 72%, of them.

What are we to make of this class? For 41 of the 50 minutes Professor Wade conducts some sort of full-class recitation or lecture. If we do not count the students' reading aloud of the essay, Professor Wade has 86% of the lines of transcript. From what he says and does, we can infer certain of his ideas about discourse and the teaching of it: that "kinds" of writing exist and that they have identifiable "structures," that some are important to teach, that they may be taught by revealing their "structure" so that novice writers may adopt it, that the substantive content of writing may be legitimately dealt with in the writing classroom, that there is a need to assess student learning and understanding at relatively frequent intervals (the seat work that he inspects, the assignment that he gives for the next day—to analyze the structure of another student-written essay), and so forth.

Surely, much of what Professor Wade does will be familiar to readers of this book. Depending on our various biases, we could readily comment on almost any of what he does. To gain greater perspective, let us look at a second case, one that even at first view appears to contrast with the first in certain major respects.

Case 2

The second example is from a senior high school class taught by another highly experienced teacher whom I shall call Mr. Gow. He is concerned that his college-bound class be able to interpret material, present their interpretations, and support them convincingly, using appropriate evidence. His students will use this kind of writing frequently during the year. What follows is the first class in a sequence that he expects to run for 2 to 3 weeks. At the beginning of the hour, he spends 2 minutes on administrative tasks. Then he begins a dialogue:

> Mr. Gow: OK. Today we are going to begin work, serious work on interpretation, writing about interpretations, and supporting them. The point will be to explain your interpretation and convince someone that it makes sense. So I'm distributing an etching by John Gilray, a late-18th-century artist. (He distributes as he talks. Students laugh as they receive the picture.) The picture is entitled *A Voluptuary under the Horrors of Digestion*. I want you to look at this really carefully and tell me what you see. (He finishes distributing the pictures.) OK, What do you see? What made you laugh?
>
> Henry: The guy is a real slob. His belly is hanging out, his buttons are popping, and he has just finished a big meal, and he's picking his teeth with his fork.
>
> Mr. Gow: What do you see? (indicating another student)
>
> Helen: It looks like there are empty wine bottles under the table and he's got a corkscrew. Is that a corkscrew hanging from that chain (referring to a watch fob)?

The students, under Mr. Gow's direction, point out a number of details in the picture: dice on the floor, slips of paper that read "Debts of Honor," bones falling off the dinner table, a chamber pot that appears to be overflowing, s stand with little bottles that Mr. Gow explains are medicine for indigestion, a coat of arms on the wall consisting of a knife and fork crossed on a plate under three feathers (Mr. Gow explains that the feathers are an emblem of the Prince of Wales, the heir to the English throne), and so forth.

> Mr. Gow: That's great. What do you think Gilray is getting at?
>
> Henry: Well, he's like saying that the guy is a slob, you know like that he eats too much, and drinks and gambles.

MR. GOW: Why do you say he eats too much?

KATHLEEN: His clothes are about to burst off him. His legs are gigantic. It looks like you could rest a wine glass on his stomach. And he obviously eats till he is sick and then eats more. What is a voluptuary anyway?

MR. GOW: That's a person who engages in the pursuit of pleasure. What are this man's pleasures, besides eating?

STUDENTS: Gambling. Drinking.

MR. GOW: You haven't said anything about his expression. What does that tell you?

STUDENT: The guy is falling asleep. Like after eating all that he would fall asleep.

KATHLEEN: I think he's sneering at somebody. Like he thinks he is really a big deal, better than anyone else.

MR. GOW: What makes you say that?

KATHLEEN: His eyes and the way his mouth is.

MR. GOW: What about them?

Students provide several details about the lips curling and the eyelids drooping. Someone suggests that he is just drunk. A debate over this interpretation ensues. Then Mr. Gow asks his earlier question:

MR. GOW: OK. Let me ask again, what do you think the point of this picture is?

JONATHAN: The guy who is supposed to become king is not fit to be king. All he does is eat, drink, and be merry. He even has a coat of arms to show how much he thinks of eating. He does that so much that he gets sick. He gambles and has debts from that. He probably doesn't care about anyone but himself. Gilray is just showing all these vices he has and saying he shouldn't be king.

Mr. Gow compliments students on their ideas about the Gilray engraving and proceeds to the next project:

What we're going to do now is look at two engravings by a famous 18th-century artist named Hogarth, William Hogarth. I think you'll find these two pieces pretty interesting. . . . I want you to work in your regular groups. Wait, don't move yet. Let me explain what I want you to do. You are coming to these cold. I am not going to tell you what is going on or what I think is going on or what Hogarth has in mind. Not yet, anyway. So your job in your group is to look at these very carefully. Pay attention to the details to see what they suggest Hogarth is getting at. Then think about what the two have in common and how they differ. After a while I'll ask you to say to the class what you think Hogarth's point is and to explain how you know. If these look strange to you, that's OK. Just use what you know and what you see to figure out what is going on. I'm going to ask four groups to tape-record today. OK? OK, let's do it.

Students move into groups of three or four in less than a minute. Mr. Gow distributes reproductions of Hogarth's *Gin Lane* and *Beer Street* to each student. Students immediately begin to examine the engravings, which are reproduced without the verses normally found at the bottom.

KEVIN: Is this guy hanging himself here? Up at the right corner? (The students have turned immediately to *Gin Lane*.)

LIZ: Right corner.

KEVIN: Yeah. This guy's hanging himself right here.

LIZ: Oh, I didn't see him. Yeah. It looks like he's hanging there.

JIM: Yeah. I like the, like the building falling down over here.

LIZ: You like that? [laughs]

KEVIN: Fights are going on.

JIM: Exactly. Like how little respect, she has more respect for whatever she has in her hand.

LIZ: Whatever it is she's drinking maybe? Than she has for her baby—

JIM: Than she does for her—

KEVIN: Cuts all over the place.

JIM: The dog eating with the guy with the bone (inaudible).

MR. GOW: I didn't tell you this and I should have. These two drawings were issued as a pair.

KEVIN: This one's like the other side of the city. Do you see what I'm saying?

LIZ: Oh yeah.

KEVIN: But the other side's beautiful. Oh, I see. Oh. I understand. The rich living next to the poor. But ignore each other at the same time.

LIZ: This one they're all. . . .

JIM: Yeah, I think Kev's got it.

LIZ: You could drop (inaudible).

JIM: I know what you're saying, yeah.

LIZ: Dealing with art. Painting.

JIM: Yeah, because this one guy, in the other one he's got, he's like holding a really big key to the city like they're worried about security and stuff, money (inaudible).

LIZ: Painting, all these antique things this guy's holding. A bunch of books.

JIM: So, yeah, over here they're worried about, they're really worried about what's going on. They're more worried about the luxury of life

"Gin Lane." Engraving by William Hogarth. Courtesy Yale Center for British Art, Paul Mellon Collection.

"Beer Street." Engraving by William Hogarth. Courtesy Yale Center for British Art, Yale University Art Gallery, The Frederick Benjamin Kaye Memorial Collection.

(referring to *Beer Street*), and over here they're more worried about just surviving (referring to *Gin Lane*).

KEVIN: This one they're building and this one's destroying.

LIZ: Everything's falling apart over here and they're building up. People building.

JIM: Yeah. And also you can tell this side's more educated because they have like all the books over in the corner.

LIZ: Yeah.

(long pause)

LIZ: What is this here? Can you read that?

KEVIN: No.

LIZ: I don't know, what do you think?

KEVIN: Something drunk or something. Something dead over here, dead drunk or something.

JIM: Yeah, I can't read what (inaudible). This is kind of ironic because it is where everything is being destroyed they have a gin royal. That's kind of ironical.

LIZ: Yeah, but they're drinking over here too.

JIM: Right.

MR. GOW: This above the door, you're trying to read that?

LIZ: Yeah.

MR. GOW: Can you read it? It says, "Drunk for a penny. Dead drunk for two pence," and then it says, "Clean straw for nothing."

KEVIN: It looks like the same building.

LIZ: What?

JIM: Yeah. I was trying to figure out. It's like seeing over here, you have like the three, the ball, the wind vane all over? You can see the top of the wind vane, that's what I'm trying to figure out as far as the relationship of these pictures to each other.

Although it is not appropriate to analyze this discussion in detail, it is interesting that it begins with students' simply noting what they see but that within a dozen lines they begin to interpret what they see. This mode of noting details and interpreting continues throughout the discussion. However, in his lines immediately above, Jim pushes the level of thinking up a notch to "the relationship of these pictures to each other."

This discussion continues for approximately 20 minutes, with Mr. Gow making six visits to the group above and about the same to each of the others. In the group above he has only 9% of the transcript lines and about the same in the other groups, leaving the students with 90% or more. After 20 minutes, Mr. Gow addresses the class as a whole:

MR. GOW: OK. Let's—you seem to have run out of steam there a little bit. Let's see what you guys think about it. Do you want to just tell us what you think? Who volunteers to tell from this group?

JULIE: OK. This is kind of like two different sides of town. In one part, because they prefer to drink gin, they lead, they are in poverty. They need to sell their things to a pawnbroker so that they can buy gin. And I'm not sure that was because it was more expensive maybe or I'm not sure about that but it has a different effect than the beer on the other side of the town. And when they're drinking beer, these people have plenty to eat, have lots of food, and they have pawnbrokers out of business, they don't need to, they don't need him to trade in things that they've got. They've got power of the government and the important people on this side. In the background are the important people going down the street.

MR. GOW: Good. What would you add to that?

STUDENT: Add to that? I would say the first one is before. They first get into drinking and think it's fun and they have plenty and there's nothing to worry about, but after a while, this one would seem to be after. They get into the gin stage and they can't stop themselves, and they have to rob graves just to get the gin.

MR. GOW: Do you all agree with that? Over here, you think this is before or after? They start out with beer and graduate to gin, is that right?

KEVIN: Hunhuh. No, like things are fine in Beer St. and terrible in Gin Lane. But that doesn't mean that beer leads to gin.

MR. GOW: (Referring to the two positions) . . . Let's say you were to take either one of those hypotheses, and you were arguing that these (holding up pictures) were related in a very specific way, either way you've got to make a specific statement about it, about the two pictures. One way to support that would be to point to the contrasts and similarities in the two pictures. There are a lot of them. What are some of the ones you've talked about already?

STUDENT: Lots of differences in the pawnbrokers' buildings . . . (inaudible).

MR. GOW: OK, and how would you, if you were writing about it, what would you say about it? Say I hadn't seen it and you were trying to explain the picture.

STUDENT: Those people who drink gin need to—

MR. GOW: Just the condition, not the cause of it.

STUDENT: In one instance you have a lot of power and you have a lot of business, and the pawnbroker is not doing well.

MR. GOW: OK. And in the other, the other pawnbroker's, what's that building like?

STUDENT: It looks like it's in pretty good condition.

MR. GOW: Yeah. It's certainly not falling apart and the sign is upright and it stays there. . . . OK. If you look at those, if you put them side by side the contrast is very sharp.

STUDENT: The pawnbroker building is in contrast to the surroundings.

MR. GOW: Good point! Do you want to explain that?

LIZ: In the picture where everything's falling apart the pawnbroker's office looks [like it's in good condition] and then in the one where everything else is built well or under construction this building is falling apart.

MR. GOW: You were talking about, this is something I heard you say, Jim, you were talking about the instruments of trade. Do you want to comment on that? Is there a contrast between the two pictures on that?

JIM: Like on Beer Street, like I said everybody like has, one guy has a file like I was saying, the other guy has a pliers and the other guy has a stick with a chain coming off it that looks like something that they have jobs and they have ways of making money in order to prosper, whereas in the Gin Street they're, you know, they're like delivering dead bodies instead of delivering a service. Like the one guy is dying, and they're just giving him gin and stuff, and they're taking the other guy, you know, they don't really have like crafts jobs, they have survival jobs. Not even jobs, just survival. Kev brought up a good point how they, how in the one there's like on Gin Street there's the animals, and like he said, instead of, if he'd elaborate on that.

KEVIN: It seemed like they'd lowered themselves to dogs by following their instinct instead of intelligence. Just going for what they want instead of what they should want.

For the next few minutes, students point out other contrasting features of the two pictures, and Mr. Gow continues to call for details and explanations. As the class nears the end, he halts the discussion and makes an assignment, asking them "to make a list of as many things as you can that have similarities and differences in the two pictures that we haven't already talked about." He tells the students, "This will prepare for some writing later."

UNPACKING ASSUMPTIONS

There are many similarities and differences between the two classes described above. First, both teachers appear to believe that students can garner appropriate knowledge for learning to write in classrooms. However, there appear to be profound differences in understandings about how that knowledge can be acquired and what it should be. Second, both devise specific means of instruction to convey that knowledge, but the instruction in the two classes is quite different. Third, what is taught in each class reflects criteria that will be used in judging the effect of the instruction, but the criteria are very different.

Professor Wade clearly believes that knowledge of the "structure" of the kind of writing is a first-order requirement. Such knowledge is implicitly understood to be reflected in the student's ability to outline a paper using the convention of the "chicken foot" outline. If students can do this, they will be able to produce the form desired. The ability to identify the parts of someone else's production becomes identified with the ability to produce a piece of writing of that kind, an extremely old idea, dating from the classical academies of Greece, in which aspiring rhetors were required to memorize the products of established speakers.

Mr. Gow, on the other hand, is clearly not so interested in having students study models of other writers' productions as he is in having them engage in the kinds of strategies that he perceives as underlying the writing tasks at hand, in this case, what we might call "interpreting and defending." For Mr. Gow, interpreting receives prime time emphasis. Over 95% of the class is taken up with interpreting specific artistic works.

He says that his students have to learn to interpret and to argue their interpretations. "For my money," he says, "the best way to learn that is to do it. You can help them in a lot of ways. You can show them how by doing it yourself. You can give them easy material to deal with before more difficult material. But you have to help them get into interpreting at some level or other. Then you can nudge them along to more sophisticated insights. What the kids were saying about the drawings towards the end of class was a lot more sophisticated than what they were saying at the beginning." He continues, "What I'm after is just what Liz did with the pawnbroker's place. Jim did it with the tools. Wasn't that great? These have been my favorite Hogarths for a long time, and I never thought of it. And that idea of Kevin's was damn good too. Maybe part of what they have to learn is confidence in their own ideas."

As far as Mr. Gow is concerned, the discourse knowledge can wait. "They need," he says, "to be competent with the content first. Once they feel confident about interpreting, then we can deal with the formal characteristics of the writing." To learn those characteristics, Mr. Gow says, he will have his students read pieces written by professionals and former students. "You can learn a lot from a piece of writing if you examine it carefully. My kids need that. They need to know the conventions of the kind of writing. But you can't learn to do that kind of interpretation simply by reading what others have done. You have to do it."

The difference here suggests another, more profound difference, an epistemological one. Professor Wade appears to have much in common with an ancient tradition of teaching that says teaching is tantamount to telling. If one tells or gives students appropriate information, their learning will indicate that they have received the information and made use of it. Through much of the 18th, 19th, and even 20th centuries, teachers of English, as well as of other subjects, believed that with proper grammar, people could, in Lindley Murray's 1795 phrase, "transfuse . . . sentiments into the minds of one another" (1849, p. 5). That is, knowledge could be conveyed directly through words and could be apprehended directly by anyone having adequate facility in the language. Such a model has epistemological implications, namely that knowledge is objective and may be acquired directly through words and the senses. This telling may take place through a textbook, a lecture, recitation, or visual demonstrations. Although this model is often referred to as teaching by transmission, I will refer to it as *objectivist* to emphasize its epistemological implications.

Mr. Gow's teaching suggests an entirely different epistemological stance, one in which anything learned must necessarily pass through the filters of past experience, through what Gadamer (1976) calls our prejudices, knowledge that allows us to recognize what is new to us, but which, at the same time, necessarily construes what we apprehend. As many have argued, from Kohler (1959) on, our sensations must be interpreted in terms of what we already know. Such a notion denies that knowledge is objective and may be acquired directly through the senses. Instead, it requires a constructivist conception of learning: namely, that what is learned may only be learned in terms of what we already know and that learners must construct what is to be learned for themselves.

One similarity between the two teachers is their pedagogical assumption that specific means can be adopted for conveying the required knowledge for writing, that teachers can be proactive (rather than simply reactive) in helping students learn to write. At the same time, the particular means that they adopt are quite different, the most obvious difference being the amount of talk time for students and teacher. If teaching is defined as the teacher's telling, one might expect the teacher to dominate the available time by wide margins. By the same token, we might expect a constructivist stance to provide more talk time to students during which they work out their own conceptions of whatever is to be learned. That certainly is the case here. In Professor Wade's class, the teacher has 86% of the lines of transcript, whereas students have only 14%. In Mr. Gow's class, the proportions are nearly reversed, 18% for the teacher and 82% for the students.

These similarities and differences suggest only some of the dimensions along which teacher thinking and action may be examined. In addition, we need to ask questions such as the following:

- What is the nature of teachers' conceptions of the subject matter to be taught?
- How may teachers' decisions about what to teach be influenced by their ideas about students as learners?

- How do conceptions of teaching and learning influence these?
- How are teachers' evaluations of their own teaching, their reflective practice, influenced by all of these?
- How can we think about the categories and processes of teachers' thinking so that we can begin to understand better how they relate to observed differences in classroom behavior?

These are the primary questions of this book. To answer them, I will attempt to combine both qualitative and quantitative methods in the comparative and contrastive study of 20 teachers of writing, 19 of them at the community college level and one at the high school level. A major goal of this study will be to explore these and other dimensions of the knowledge that is essential for teaching.

THE PLAN OF THE PRESENT STUDY

The major question for this book, then, has to do with teacher knowledge and its relationship to classroom events that are directed toward learning outcomes. Put another way, What are the decisions that teachers make to bring about learning in their students and why do they make them?

Since the questions raised here are concerned with learning, they must also be concerned with something to be learned. I have selected the teaching of writing because, I readily admit, writing has been one of my major research and pedagogical interests for many years. Given this focus, the goal will be to construct a theoretical model that attempts to explicate the kinds of knowledge involved in teaching; the character, quality, and interactions of such knowledge; and their operation in practice. To this end, I will try to bring three general sources of information to bear on the problem: studies of the teaching of writing that provide the grounds for beginning to delineate categories of teacher knowledge (Chapter 2); studies of teacher thinking; an extensive study of 19 teachers of writing in a large urban community college system; and an examination of one high school teacher.

In Chapter 2, I examine current thinking about pedagogical content knowledge, a concept that has been developed to some degree by Shulman (1986, 1987) and his students (e.g., Grossman, 1990). I argue that for the concept to be useful it must be examined in enough detail to provide insight into the critical assumptions that determine classroom experiences of students. In addition, I look at the problem of how to analyze classroom activity in order to come to some understanding of the kinds of knowledge and reflection that are part of it. I argue, in particular, for the necessity of examining actual classroom actions and the macro- and microcurricula in which they occur. I then turn to the means of analyzing classroom events and the kinds of knowledge that those events represent. These considerations provide a framework for examining both teachers' subject matter knowledge and their pedagogical content knowledge.

In Chapter 3, I explicate the design of the present study of teacher thinking and action in writing classrooms. I present key quantitative results of this analysis, including central tendencies for the group of 19 community college teachers. These results provide the basis for separating out what may be called different profiles of teaching and open the way for the exploration of the connection of thinking to action and change.

In Chapter 4, I examine cases that turn on certain knowledge or attitudes concerning students, primarily their ability or inability to learn. I ask how this knowledge appears to interact with knowledge of goals and knowledge of content. The chapter includes two contrasting cases, one teacher who is optimistic and one who is not. The teachers in both cases display a high reliance on teaching discourse knowledge through lecture. At the same time, these cases provide insight into different conceptions of the goals of the writing class, of the knowledge necessary for writing, and of pedagogical practice and how these result in different experiences for students.

I continue in Chapter 5 with this analysis, but take the focus to different assumptions about teaching and learning and to substantive knowledge for writing rather than discourse knowledge.

In Chapter 6, I examine the concept of curriculum in the exploration of two teachers, both of whom construct curricula rather than simply adopt it from some outside source. Here I examine how various parts of teacher knowledge influence this construction.

In Chapter 7, I turn to the ideas of epistemological stance, the categories of teacher knowledge, and their organization, in an effort to develop a theoretical model of teacher knowledge toward which in the earlier chapters I have been driving.

In Chapter 8, I examine the implications of this model for reflective practice, teacher change, and further research. More specifically, I examine the ways in which teachers' epistemological stances, constructions of knowledge about students, and constructions of subject matter appear to promote or inhibit reflective activity of the kind that results in changes in teaching at the micro and macro levels. I examine what this combination implies for teacher change and conclude with implications for research.

❧ 2 ❧

Knowledge in Classrooms

IN HER DEFINITION OF pedagogical content knowledge Grossman (1990) expands somewhat on Shulman's (1986, 1987) earlier statements. She includes the following: (a) "knowledge and beliefs about the purposes for teaching a subject at different grade levels," (b) "knowledge of students' understanding, conceptions, and misconceptions of particular topics in a subject matter," (c) "knowledge of curriculum materials available for teaching particular subject matter" and knowledge about the horizontal and vertical curricular structures for that subject matter (p. 8), and (d) "knowledge of instructional strategies and representations for teaching particular topics" (p. 9). Several of these subcategories have a clear relationship to Shulman's noncontent knowledge: general pedagogy, curricula, students, and ends and purposes.

One might guess that these categories do not exist independently. If one brings knowledge of students to bear on what is to be taught, one would expect it to influence decisions about the actual selections of goals and materials for teaching. One would further expect that, in the process of teaching, teachers would have cause to reconsider goals when they note that the students are having difficulty, or to change the teaching strategies, materials, activities, or feedback. Such reconsideration or reflection is what Schön (1987) calls reflection in action.

My purpose in this book is to examine these categories of knowledge to determine the nature of their relevance to an individual teacher's knowledge and the impact of that knowledge on classroom events. For if the knowledge has no impact on events, then it will be arguably of little use to those of us concerned with the nature of teaching and how it makes a difference to students.

A key problem confronting any effort to describe a teacher's knowledge is the problem of how we can begin to understand what teachers know. If teachers tell us what they know about teaching, can we assume that what they tell is what they know? Or can we assume that what they tell us is what they do? If the work of teachers is to develop knowledge in their students, how is such knowledge manifest in classrooms? These are important questions in understanding and conceptualizing teacher knowledge because a significant part of teacher knowledge may be in performance. That is, their performance may reveal what they know more than what they say.

22

KNOWLEDGE IN PERFORMANCE

In his devastating repudiation of the Cartesian separation of mind from body, of thought from action, Gilbert Ryle, the distinguished longtime professor of metaphysical philosophy at Oxford, argues that this metaphoric separation gives rise to a concept of mind that is tantamount to what he calls the "dogma of the Ghost in the Machine" (1984, pp. 15–16). In this conception of mind, Ryle argues,

> [t]here is a polar opposition between mind and matter, an opposition which is often brought out as follows. Material objects are situated in a common field, known as "space," and what happens to one body in one part of space is mechanically connected with what happens to other bodies in other parts of space. But mental happenings occur in insulated fields, known as "minds", and there is . . . no direct causal connection between what happens in one mind and what happens in another. (p. 13)

Ryle argues that the separation of mind from body or of thought from action is entirely wrong "in principle." It is a "category mistake" that arises from the unwarranted assumption that the concepts of mind and body are of the same order of existence. Ryle argues that conjunctions of mind and body or of mental and physical processes are absurd because their manner of existence is not parallel. Such absurd conjunctions are frequently seen as jests or satiric commentaries, for example, "She came home in a flood of tears and a sedan chair" (p. 22).

If we accept this conjunction, if we turn to *thought* and then to *action*, we in effect separate them. We count them as different, but parallel, and treat them in order, usually with thought as the necessary precursor of action, the former giving rise to the latter. I will not attempt to summarize Ryle's (1984) argument except to point out that such conjunction is unable to explicate intelligent performance for which the performer cannot explain the rules that govern its actions. The easiest example is our tacit knowledge of grammar, which enables native speakers to order words in standard ways without being able to articulate the rules they follow. Native speakers of English, for example, place a series of adjectives in a particular order without being able to articulate the precise rules for doing it. As Hartwell (1985) has shown, native speakers informed of the rules, and asked to follow them, experience great difficulty in doing so.

Or consider Ryle's (1984) commentary on an argument delivered by a skilled arguer. Ryle points out that much of the argument will never have been constructed before. He (or she) will have to deal with new evidence and objections, and pull together elements in the new situation that had not "been previously coordinated":

> In short, he has to innovate, and where he is innovating, he is not operating from habit. . . . That he is now thinking what he is doing is shown not only by this fact that he is operating without precedents, but also by the fact that he is ready to recast his expression of obscurely put points, on guard against ambiguities or else on the

lookout for chances to exploit them, taking care not to rely on easily refutable inferences, alert in meeting objections and resolute in steering the general course of his
reasoning in the direction of his final goal. (p. 47)

The point is that such intelligent performances cannot be planned in advance
except in the most general ways. The arguer may plan to concentrate on the purpose of the argument, keeping in mind the sets of data available and so on. But he
or she cannot attend to all the rules involved. Further, such performers may be
unable to explain afterwards all the rules they followed in performance.

Is the mind on vacation during such performances? Ryle (1984) would argue that it is certainly not. It is simply not at liberty to be on vacation because it is
not a separate entity. It must be part of the performance, in union with those parts
of the body that execute the performance. "Overt intelligent performances are not
clues to the working of minds; they are those workings" (p. 58).

All of this is not to say that skilled performers are not concerned with standards, or have no use for criteria, or cannot provide explanations at some level of
what they do. On the contrary, such criteria govern performance and make self-
correction possible.

If all this is true, what does it have to say about the analysis of teaching and
teacher knowledge? First, it implies very clearly that an examination of what has
been called teacher thinking that is undertaken in isolation from a detailed analysis of what teachers do is bound to be limited at best. As is true of other thoughtful performers, teachers may be unable to verbalize all that is associated with what
they do. Kernel ideas mentioned only in passing in a verbal account may be explicated in practice. We should expect to find ideas and beliefs about practice
embedded in the actions of practice. On the other hand, if we watch only the classroom practice, without being privy to the commentary of the teacher, we will be
unable to understand the intentions and assumptions underlying the performance.
Therefore, to better understand teaching, it will be necessary to examine both what
teachers do and what they say about it.

KNOWLEDGE IN CLASSROOMS

We frequently think of the knowledge of classrooms as the knowledge represented
in the curriculum, Grossman's (1990) third category of pedagogical content knowledge, "knowledge of curriculum materials available for teaching particular subject matter" and knowledge about the "horizontal and vertical curricula for a subject" (p. 8). This category of knowledge represents the larger structures of a
curriculum, what we might call the macrocurriculum. She says, for example, that
English teachers "draw upon their knowledge of which books and topics are typically addressed in the ninth grade and how the various strands of a ninth grade

curriculum might be organized" (p. 8). This language strongly suggests that Grossman has in mind the kind of planning within a subject matter area that we find in scope and sequence outlines, which are often composed by committee. Thus, a ninth-grade curriculum committee might indicate units on the short story, poetry, drama, and the novel as appropriate. Ordinarily that means that teachers are expected to include those kinds of literature. However, teachers have considerable flexibility within the structure. The teacher is likely to have considerable discretion over which short stories to assign and how to treat them. Indeed, although teachers may agree about the macrocurriculum, about what topics or works to teach, the experience of students working within the macrocurriculum may differ widely because of the differences in the ways in which teachers handle those topics and works. To understand the differences in the kinds of knowledge manifest in classrooms, it is necessary to examine the fine grain of the microcurriculum.

Imagine, for example, a different version of Mr. Gow's class presented in Chapter 1. It is conceivable that another teacher might have used the same engravings, *Gin Lane* and *Beer Street*, in quite different ways. Another teacher might have felt that group work was a waste of time in which the "blind lead the blind" in considering artistic productions that are quite out of the experience of students. In the name of efficiency and superior knowledge, this teacher might well have decided to conduct a discussion him- or herself, in which he or she could guide the students in their understanding of the Hogarth prints. If the teacher is like most teachers studied by Goodlad (1984) and more recently by Nystrand, Gamoran, Kachur, & Prendergast (1997), the discussion is likely to be what Nystrand calls monologic talk, mostly by the teacher, who has most of the lines and whose questions to students are quizlike, with no necessary connections of one to the next. As Nystrand et al. point out, these questions "require students to recall what someone else thought, not to articulate, examine, elaborate, or revise what they themselves thought" (p. 3). In our observations student responses to these questions serve as platforms for the instructor to present information and interpretations. In this imaginary class, our teacher, whom I will call Mr. Lector, might ask students a question about *Beer Street*, such as, "What implements do the people here have in their possession?" He would wait briefly as students scan the print for implements. Upon receiving even one response, such as "pliers," he would proceed to provide the interpretation that Jim did in Mr. Gow's class. Perhaps Mr. Lector would ask another question about implements in the possession of the inhabitants of *Gin Lane*. If a student provided a response such as "glasses and bottles," he would proceed to compare the two prints from that perspective, leading to many of the same conclusions that Jim's group developed in Mr. Gow's class. He might then ask some questions about the pawnbroker establishments in the two prints (in *Gin Lane* the pawnshop prospers, along with the gin mill, distillery, and coffin-maker's shop; in *Beer Street* it is crumbling) and proceed to interpret that difference for the students, as Liz did. In our observations many teachers used just such a structure, referring to it as *discussion*.

Mr. Gow opens his class with a teacher-led discussion (see Chapter 1), but the structure of that discussion is quite different. At first, he asks students to tell what details they see in the picture. Many of these require some explication. Let us turn to a specific example that opens with a student's question:

BILL: What's this thing behind him, on that little stand, kind of like a pot?

MR. GOW: What is that? Does anyone have an idea about that?

LILLIAN: Isn't that a chamber pot?

STUDENT: What's that?

LILLIAN: It's like, for going to the toilet. You know, before they had toilets, like indoor plumbing.

(There is a general sound of disgust, "Eeeugh! Yuk!")

CATHY: It's right there by the table. That's awful!

BILL: And it's overflowing, isn't it?

JIM: Yeah, but that's not . . . uh . . . uh, excrement, I don't think. Because, it's not . . . like dark.

MR. GOW: What do you make of that? Any ideas? (After a pause, Mr. Gow continues.) In the Middle Ages, castles had little rooms off their main dining halls called vomitoriums. These were used during big meals, you know, 15 courses, so that people could uhm, purge themselves after a few courses and then go back to the table and eat a few more.

BILL: You mean, like this guy eats, throws up, then eats again?

JIM: That would make sense why the pot's overflowing.

CATHY: That is so disgusting. What kind of, what kind of pleasure . . . Didn't we say that *voluptuary* means somebody that wants pleasure. What kind of pleasure does eating and throwing up give you? That just doesn't make any sense.

LIZ: It's like some people drink and drink and drink for pleasure, and they get drunk and fall down and throw up all over themselves. (There is subdued laughter.) So look at the title, "A Voluptuary under the Horrors of Digestion." This guy wants pleasure and ends up with horror. It makes sense. Do you see what I'm saying? Like, either he eats so much he gets sick or he gets sick on purpose so he can eat more.

JIM: Maybe both.

Nystrand and his colleagues (1997) would explain the differences in these two bits of classroom dialogue as the difference between monologic and dialogic.

In Mr. Lector's monologic class, students are restricted to indicating bits of information through questions that are unauthentic by virtue of the fact that Mr. Lector already knows the answers. Because students simply supply responses to these very limited questions, what they say has nothing to do with what their peers say. Their responses are not contingent upon one another. They simply provide a stepping-stone for Mr. Lector to follow. Mr. Lector provides the students with all the knowledge, and it is declarative. That is, he simply gives students his interpretation of the pictures.

In contrast, in Mr. Gow's class, discussion of the chamber pot begins with a student question reinforced by Mr. Gow, whose question is authentic because he does not know if his students know about such things. Later, he asks, "What do you make of that?" The question is authentic, calling for the students' own interpretations. The students' responses become the center of attention. Nystrand et al. (1997) would say that Mr. Gow validates the students' responses by allowing them to affect "the subsequent course of the discussion" (p. 19). In this case, the student responses do not simply affect the subsequent course of the discussion, they *are* the discussion. Further, in Nystrand's words, the responses are "sequentially contingent," and only then, in Bakhtin's (1981) theory, do "understandings develop" (p. 19). Nystrand et al. argue convincingly that this kind of instruction results in superior learning (cf. 1997, pp. 28–29 and 70–71).

These two examples, one real and one based on real cases, display profound differences in pedagogical content knowledge. Consider the differences in the kinds of knowledge conveyed. In Mr. Lector's episodes the knowledge remains declarative, knowledge of *what*. There is no attempt to help students develop their own interpretation or analyses. The knowledge in Mr. Lector's class is essentially static. It is presented, and then it floats in the air of the classroom. Whether anyone breathes it in and uses it is essentially out of the teacher's control.

In the Mr. Gow episode, on the other hand, students do nearly all the developing of knowledge. They transform relatively simple observations into complex interpretations of what they see. As students develop those interpretations, they not only learn them, but also learn how to develop them. In addition to gaining declarative knowledge, they gain procedural knowledge, knowledge of *how* to do things. This is Ryle's (1984) knowledge of *how*.

What does all this indicate regarding the existence of knowledge in classrooms? Does it exist in the heads of the participants? Ryle (1984) has argued convincingly that such notions are misleading. Does it exist in the books and maps and drawings that may fill the shelves and cover the bulletin boards? I prefer to think it exists in the actions of individuals, actions that need not be overt, but, as Ryle points out, may include talking or imagining inside oneself. If we view the classroom as a place of learning and see knowledge as existing in the actions of the participants, then declarative knowledge emanating from one individual in the form of lecture or performance can only be activated for the others if they some-how work to transform it.

Curiously, though the level of declarative and procedural knowledge in class-rooms varies from teacher to teacher, all of our writing teachers evaluate their students on the basis of their written products, products that necessarily reflect the acquisition of procedural knowledge. That is, even when writing classrooms manifest only declarative knowledge, teachers still evaluate their students, not on recall of what the teachers have said in class, but on the ability of the students to transform that declarative knowledge into the procedures that enable them to pro-duce effective writing.

Some teachers tell their classes that they want them to learn *how* to perform the operations involved in various types of writing and try to help them do so. Mr. Gow announces such a purpose to his class (see Chapter 1): "Today we are going to begin work, serious work on interpretation, writing about interpretations, and supporting them." This statement makes clear that the major goal for several days will be developing, defending, and writing about interpretations. It implies how the evaluation might proceed. "The point will be to explain your interpretation and convince someone that it makes sense." In Mr. Gow's class, the knowledge in the group work and in the teacher-led discussion has two major parts: the inter-pretation largely constructed by the students and the knowledge of procedures students learn as they construe them. Mr. Gow is not concerned with particular interpretations. For him, the important knowledge is how to interpret and defend the interpretations. He says,

> You can help them in a lot of ways. You can show them how by doing it yourself. You can give them easy material to deal with before more difficult material. But you gotta help them get into interpreting at some level or other. Then you sort of nudge them along to more sophisticated insights. What the kids were saying about the drawings towards the end of class was a lot more sophisticated than what they were saying at the beginning.

The essence of procedural knowledge lies in what the students do in class. It is learning *how*. Therein lies the evaluation. Mr. Gow listens to what the students say to evaluate his teaching. Does the activity engender interpretations? Are they adequate interpretations? At the end of the class he is very happy with the stu-dents (see Chapter 1). He says,

> What I'm after is just what Liz did with the pawnbroker's place. Jim did it with the tools. Wasn't that great?! These have been my favorite Hogarths for a long time, and I never thought of it. And that idea of Kevin's was damn good too.

Teachers, such as our fictitious Mr. Lector, also say that they want students to learn how to develop certain kinds of writing. But they do not use classroom time to engage students in the tasks. Rather, they tell them about what is to be done. In these classes, it is up to the students to make the transformation of declarative to procedural knowledge.

Classroom knowledge, however, has additional dimensions. In writing classrooms, knowledge is likely to include that about discourse, the substance of writing, and the general processes of writing, at the very least. Discourse knowledge, for our purposes, may be usefully divided into knowledge at the level of the whole and knowledge at the level of syntax and mechanics. The first includes both formal features of "types" of writing, organizational principles, and rhetorical features of the whole written discourse, whereas the second includes knowledge of syntax, usage, and conventions or mechanics. By substantive knowledge, I mean the subject matter about which someone writes.

Any of these may be treated as knowledge of *what* or knowledge of *how*, as declarative or procedural knowledge. Reading models of certain types of writing or hearing the rules governing their structure amounts to declarative knowledge of discourse. Activities involving the manipulation or generation of such types amount to procedural knowledge related to discourse. Listening to a lecture or reading about the content to be used in writing to show what one knows (the major function of writing in Britton, Burgess, Martin, McLeod, & Rose, 1975) entails declarative knowledge of substance. Activities involving the manipulation or transformation of content for writing, as in the students' interpretations in Mr. Gow's class, amount to procedural knowledge. Mr. Gow's students are learning the procedures that they can use in their later interpretations of other materials. In addition, students may focus on knowledge of general writing processes (prewriting, drafting, revising, providing feedback, editing, and so forth), and even these may be treated as declarative or procedural knowledge.

ANALYZING KNOWLEDGE IN OBSERVED CLASSROOMS

Many writers undertake to write about classrooms using a discursive or descriptive style, often proclaiming that they eschew the analytic. This dichotomy has never been clear to me. By definition, analysis involves determining parts of wholes and the relationship of parts to one another and to the whole. Any naming of parts is inescapably analytic because it differentiates some object of perception from its field, interprets it, and categorizes it, thereby giving prominence to certain features of the object over the others. Any description must necessarily name parts and, in doing so, sets them apart from other parts. When the style is descriptive, analytic categories that are inherently part of the description more often than not remain undefined. When categories are undefined, we have no way of knowing what range of phenomena any one category encompasses, or even whether terms that are apparently quite different may incorporate comparable phenomena. Further, when a single case is presented as typical of a group of phenomena, we have no way of knowing just how typical it is. What is the distribution of the phenomenon under consideration, for the individual case described and for all cases in the sample?

For these reasons, in this study, I have undertaken both detailed qualitative analyses of individual teachers and their classes and a detailed quantitative analysis of the set of freshman composition classes taught by the 19 teachers observed, all of whom taught in a large urban community college system. The observations and postobservation interviews were collected initially to determine the extent of change in teaching practices as a result of an intensive seminar on recent research into the teaching of writing. The data collected include observer notes and audio recordings of at least 3 hours of classroom teaching in each of 2 years, interviews following observations when possible, and a 60-minute interview in which teachers were asked about their general views of the course taught, their goals, the materials used, the kinds of activities included, the nature of the students in the class, the teachers' views of their teaching situations, and reasons underlying their teaching decisions. These questions on major topics were followed, as necessary, by probes to elicit more specific information. In interviews following observations, the teachers were asked specific questions about goals, materials, activities of the sessions observed, and the reasons underlying them.

Using the observer notes and audio recordings, researchers analyzed the pedagogical content of the 127 hours of observed classes at the level of episode, defined by changes in one or more of the following: materials used, instructional goals, or teacher-class relationships. This content analysis also examines the types and character of knowledge appearing in each episode.

Identification of Episodes

Teaching does not go on as an undifferentiated flow of activity. Rather, it develops in chunks of various kinds. Even the casual observer will note that most teachers teach some things, and then the students take a test or write a composition, or do something that provides opportunities for monitoring progress. We may think of these large chunks as lessons, units, or even whole courses within a larger curriculum. But there are smaller chunks as well, chunks that I call episodes; in Mr. Gow's teaching, for example, an episode of small-group work was followed by a full-class teacher-led discussion.

These episodes are the means by which knowledge is developed in the classroom. The central problems are, What kind of knowledge do they help develop?

and, How do they develop it? Before we try to answer these questions, we must consider what episodes are, and how they may be related.

The following summary of a class taught by Professor Danziger will be helpful in answering these questions. I quote Professor Danziger occasionally to reveal how he shows the divisions to his students.

> Professor Danziger opens class by referring to the Bulwer-Lytton contest held annually at a university in California. He holds up a copy of a publication, explaining, "These are the winners from a contest. . . . These are opening lines from a novel, or novels that were never written." He calls it "marvelous, marvelous writing," reads the winning entry in the contest, and says, "Now I think you're all dying to be able to write like this. And our next assignment may take you to this goal. And we'll get into it later on tonight."
>
> Next, Professor Danziger returns papers before setting up an overhead projector and announcing that he has three papers that he thinks "would be worth looking at." He projects the first and talks about it, reading some of it aloud and commenting on a variety of features, from the quality of detail to spelling and mechanics. He follows a similar procedure with two more papers. After taking down the projector, he distributes compositions to his students, whispering comments to them as he does so, and announces that students may rewrite to improve their grades.
>
> Next, Professor Danziger says, "The best thing would be for us to get right into our paper topic. We're going to do something called the absolute phrase. And let me pass out some samples of some rather good prose." Professor Danziger reads and comments on one sentence of the passage, before putting one absolute on the board and asking what an absolute phrase is. He comments on several more absolute constructions in the excerpt before reading the remainder aloud without comment. Professor Danziger distributes a two-page handout that he says "encompasses the next paper." He selects sentences from the handout and expands them as examples of how to write absolute phrases. He explains that the next piece of writing should take off from one of the sentences supplied on the handout. He says, "This is going to be a description-loaded narrative. I want you to load the sentences down with parallel verbs, absolute phrases, parallel adjectives, or adjective phrases, usually at the end of the sentence."
>
> After a few more comments, he says, "Last thing, active/passive voice. . . . We're going to take some perfectly fine active-voice sentences and destroy them. We'll put them in the passive voice. . . . I'd like to go around and see individuals and try to do some coaching." For the next 20 minutes Professor Danziger moves around the room to individual students, helping with transformations, first from active to passive voice. Next, students work on changing "weak, wordy passive voice" verbs to active.

Episode Boundaries

As Professor Danziger works through his lesson, he announces changes. Other teachers do the same. Professor Danziger nearly always announces that something new is coming (e.g., "Here is the assignment") or that something has ended (e.g., "I think that does it," as he turns off the projector). Several of the teachers use more subtle linguistic signals, such as a phrase comparable to "OK. Now." Others are a bit more colorful: "OK, now we want to stop at another station for a minute."

Most of these announcements coincide with (1) changes in material (e.g., his change from handout on absolute phrases to the handout on passive and active voice); (2) changes in teacher-student relationships (e.g., a movement from what is essentially lecture to seat work on passive and active verbs); or (3) a major change in goals (e.g., although it does not occur here, a change from the identification of absolute phrases in a model to the creation of absolutes based on other sentences). These episode markers can be described as follows:

1. *Materials* include compositions, literary texts, audio/visual materials, and so on. Sometimes class discussions take student ideas as their focus. For example, several student ideas may be considered en masse, in a single episode. Or one student's idea for a paper may be examined in detail before the class moves to another, which is examined as a separate idea providing another episode just as would a change in material.
2. *Teacher-student relationships* also mark changes in episodes. We coded five basic types of student-teacher relationships: (a) students work in concert under the direct supervision of the teacher as in lectures and teacher-led discussions (we will call this "frontal teaching" after Goodlad, 1984); (b) students collaborate in small groups, semi-independent of the teacher; (c) students work independently on various tasks but with teacher supervising; (d) students confer with teacher alone—without other students; and (e) homework. Homework is included here because it appears to be conceptualized as an extension of the teacher's relationship with the student, one in which the student has more independence but is to prepare for something that will take place in class later or is to make use of what the teacher has taught.
3. *Changes in instructional goals* also mark episodes. We did not consider ultimate educational purposes (e.g., to promote the growth of all individuals for active participation in a democracy) that seem not to change over short lessons, but fairly specific instrumental goals (e.g., to understand Browning's "My Last Duchess"). For the most part, changes in such goals are readily detectable. But some ambiguity exists because so many relatively concrete instructional goals have subsets of goals. Thus, writing a composition is often understood as having four stages: prewriting, writing, revising, and editing. If students are simply moving through the stages in order to complete the assignment, even

if the teacher calls for revising and editing, these are most appropriately viewed as related to the same instrumental goal—writing the composition. On the other hand, if the teacher focuses attention on *how* to "prewrite," *how* to revise, or *how* to edit, and provides specific instruction in each, then each seems more usefully viewed as an end in itself, and, therefore, as a separate episode.

To the preceding guides for identifying episodes, we added a ground rule concerning the length of episodes. Teachers do many things that may shift attention from tasks at hand but that take only seconds. By our rules, a joke that lasted 15 seconds or the passing back of papers that lasted 30 seconds might arguably be identified as separate episodes. Depending on the context, however, these might also be viewed as part of the ongoing episode. We therefore decided that for an activity to be counted as a separate episode, it must last for at least 2 minutes. Thus, after Professor Danziger's first episode above, he returns some papers and again, after using the overhead to comment on the three papers, he distributes papers to students. These are management activities, but since they take place in less than a minute each, they are counted as part of the episodes to which they are linked. Similarly, writing on the board during an ongoing discussion counts as part of the ongoing activity, because it is done quickly and supports the discussion. However, when a teacher writes on the board at the beginning of class or after the initial activities, and writes for 10 or 12 minutes, as happens fairly often in some classes, we counted these interludes as separate episodes.

Given these guidelines, we can begin to think about the episodes of Professor Danziger's class. He begins with a brief introduction of descriptive writing that is intended to be amusing, followed by three episodes in each of which he partially reads and comments upon a student paper. (Although Professor Danziger treated these readings as a single episode in many ways, he signals with each switch that something new is coming, e.g., "Let's get to the next paper," and we adhered to the rule of change in material.) These three are followed by five more episodes: one examining the use of absolutes in a model, a diversionary episode of 5 minutes, a worksheet on absolutes, homework, and the episode on passive voice.

The difficult question still remains. What kinds of knowledge are involved in these episodes, and how are they related? What is their manner of existence?

The Function of Episodes

It seemed clear after our examining several classrooms that not all episodes were instructional in nature. Some seemed far removed from instruction, for example, when an instructor spends 15 minutes explaining a course that she will teach in the next semester and encouraging students to enroll. Other episodes seemed relevant to instruction but different from it. One teacher of a remedial class spent several minutes checking student notebooks to be sure that their materials were present and organized. Our research team discussed this episode from a variety of perspectives, some arguing that it had an instructional function, namely, teaching the young people how to be students. Some saw it as assessment. We finally decided to label such episodes as management, inasmuch as they supported and might be necessary for instruction, but did not actually constitute instruction in writing.

One difficulty that arose less frequently than I had expected had to do with the few episodes in which students wrote in class. These could be categorized as having to do with instruction or assessment. If the teacher went from student to student providing advice or suggestions in a workshop setting, we categorized the episode as instruction. If, however, there was no coaching, the episode counted as assessment.

Management episodes are those whose major function is to establish or maintain classroom procedures. They include taking attendance, explaining seating arrangements, discussing goals or grades, writing on the board, and so forth. We need to distinguish between these teacher tasks when they assume an importance of their own and when they are brief directions to groups or statements about grades that are usually a part of some larger episode. In Professor Danziger's class, all management is subsumed as segments in larger episodes. Distributing papers, setting up a projector, and so forth he dispatches efficiently in less than 2 minutes. Other teachers spend several minutes on any one of these, making them stand in our system as independent episodes.

Diversion episodes are those that have no apparent function in light of the course goals. They are periods of time of more than 2 minutes during which the teacher is absent from the class, talks with a colleague while the class waits, tells a story that is not relevant to the class goals, or dismisses the class early. In the class above, Professor Danziger has one diversionary episode of 5 minutes.

Classification of Knowledge in Episodes

When it came to classifying the knowledge in episodes, we attempted to come at that knowledge from two different perspectives: subject matter content and student participation.

Knowledge as Subject Matter Content. We coded the following kinds of subject matter content: *substantive* (the actual or possible content of writing); *formal-rhetorical* (knowledge related to the characteristics of writing as whole pieces of written discourse); and *syntactic-mechanical* (knowledge of syntactic structure and usage or mechanics).[1] We used a separate category for episodes that combined formal and mechanical-syntactic concerns.

The episodes of Professor Danziger's class illustrate some of these categories. He does not deal with substantive knowledge, as Mr. Gow and Mr. Lector were seen to do earlier. His first episode deals with formal features of narrative writing, namely, elaboration and specificity. The three episodes in which he comments on three student papers fall into the combination category because he deals with both formal and certain mechanical features of the writing. In the fifth episode, in which he presents a model of writing that uses absolute modifiers, his focus is again on a combination of formal and syntactic features. That is, he uses the model to illustrate the idea of elaboration and to teach absolute modifiers. The sixth episode is a diversion in which the professor tells a story unrelated to the ongoing instruction. The seventh, on absolute modifiers, involves explication of absolute modifiers with a work sheet for creating absolutes. This episode clearly falls into the category of syntactic knowledge. He assigns the work sheet as homework. In the seventh, he asks students to work on changing active voice to passive and vice versa, another example of focus on syntactic knowledge.

We have seen several episodes in which the content is what we call substantive: all episodes of Mr. Gow's class, the episode of the imaginary Mr. Lector, and the episode of Professor Wade's class in which he reports the findings of his own survey of students' preferences in the opposite sex. Knowledge of substance is likely to appear as the content of lectures or models, or even student talk about ideas or events about which people have written or may write. In many classes we see talk about the content of essays or stories.

Knowledge as Participation. Our second level of knowledge classification has to do primarily with the kind of student participation involved. When the teacher is talking, whether students are listening or not, we classify the knowledge as declarative. When students were actively engaged in investigations or in the construction of ideas, we classify the knowledge as procedural. On some occasions, instructors explained procedures, how to develop a thesis, or how to make a comparison, for example, but without engaging students in doing those. We classified these as explanations of procedures, a subset of declarative knowledge. Definitions of declarative and procedural knowledge appear above.

Instructional episodes were classified as exhibiting the teaching of procedural knowledge only when students were actually engaged in using procedures in an instructional task other than listening. In lecture-recitation, the knowledge is nearly always declarative. Students are expected to learn what the teacher says. However, if the class turns to discussion and students are engaged in building new understandings, as in the dialogic example of Mr. Gow's class earlier in this chapter, we classified the knowledge as procedural. On the other hand, if students simply vent opinions without uptake for more careful examination, we classified that knowledge as declarative.

If students were engaged in developing new understandings in collaborative group work, as in Mr. Gow's class, described in Chapter 1, the knowledge was classified as procedural. If students worked in small groups, reading their compositions aloud, but without any discussion aimed at revision or developing new ideas, in effect, simply listening to the writing of others, we classified the knowledge as declarative. If students were engaged in seat work and if the teacher was coaching individuals as they worked, as in Professor Danziger's episode on active and passive verbs, we classified the knowledge as procedural. On the other hand, if students were doing individual seat work with no coaching, the episode was classified as assessment, not instruction.

In our analysis, we found many teachers focusing on what seems to be best regarded as a subset of declarative knowledge, explanations of procedures, what amounts to statements of directions. This is the kind of knowledge that we find in the booklet that comes with a new camera or when a teacher explains how to use a procedure that will be the basis for an essay. For example, Professor James tells students how to evaluate movies and other products of popular culture, using what he calls criteria. The students do not actually evaluate; rather, they hear his explanation.

In dealing with how to evaluate a movie, he explains that one may evaluate the acting, the plot, the setting, and other features of a film. In dealing with setting, for example, he talks about the idea of setting and how to use it as a criterion:

> The film was set in [a large city], so I got a setting that we're very familiar with. Maybe you're going to evaluate that movie and you liked the fact that, hey, here's a film set where I know about something. But then there was one real weak part of the setting in the film. They attempted to simulate a snowy winter. And they dumped all this cotton on the ground and they pretended that that was winter. It was pretty unrealistic, I mean, hell, you know what winter . . . looks like. And it doesn't have a whole lot of cotton down on the ground. It has real snow that gets dirty real quick and gets slushy and makes your feet quite miserable. If you look at the setting of a movie and judge whether it was realistic or whether it was appropriate, [you are making an evaluation].

Professor James goes on to explain how to use other criteria for evaluating movies, and later, he explains how to evaluate TV shows and recordings. He engages students tangentially in his construction of how to evaluate, but they do no evaluation.

Had Professor James engaged students in the actual evaluation of a short film, using some set of true criteria, that activity would have been coded as procedural knowledge. But he does not, and we code the knowledge as explanation of procedures.

In Chapters 4, 5, 6, and 7 I will examine how these types of knowledge about writing differ in amount and type from classroom to classroom. Further, I will explore some of the factors that appear to determine this distribution.

NOTE

1. We also coded for general writing process–oriented knowledge, but the results were not productive for this study and will not be reported here.

❦ 3 ❦

Profiles of Teaching

ALTHOUGH THERE ARE MANY striking differences among the 20 teachers examined in this book, there are also many comparable tendencies among certain subgroups. In this chapter, I will examine the data obtained through observations of and interviews with the 19 community college teachers included in the sample. In particular, I will be concerned with the following questions about the character of instruction:

1. What proportion of time is spent on instruction?
2. What kinds of activities characterize the delivery or development of this knowledge?
3. What is the nature and variation of knowledge taught?
4. What factors may account for differences among teachers?

Finally, I will examine the relationship of certain of these factors to differences in classroom activities.

WHAT PROPORTION OF TIME IS SPENT ON INSTRUCTION?

During the 2 years of observations, teachers, as a group, devoted 82% of observed classroom time to teaching, about 9.6% to management (e.g., taking attendance, setting up the projector, checking the content of notebooks), about 4.4% to assessment, and 3.7% to various diversions (e.g., teacher leaves the class or is late for class, teacher announces a class on drama and encourages students to enroll). As one might expect, this pattern is not consistent across teachers. Instructional time ranges from a low of 58.5% to a high of 94%. This is an enormous variation. It means that in a semester course consisting of 48 hours of class meeting time, the students of the low-instruction teacher receive only slightly more than 28 hours of instruction, whereas the students of the high-instruction teacher receive more than 45 hours of instruction, a difference of more than 37%. The teacher with a low of 58.5% instructional time has the highest percentage of time spent on management (26.5) and the highest on diversion (15).

WHAT KINDS OF ACTIVITIES CHARACTERIZE
THE DELIVERY OF KNOWLEDGE?

During the 2 years of our observation, teachers devoted 73.4% of instructional time to what Goodlad (1984) called frontal teaching, with the teacher standing at the front of the class and directing the flow of talk either by lecturing or by asking questions that permit only limited student responses (conducting recitation). On the basis of lines of transcript (not including reading aloud by teachers or students), these teachers spoke an average of 89% of the lines in frontal teaching. It is possible for a teacher to be less dominant in frontal teaching, as when a discussion involves many students taking significant turns in the ongoing discussion, with teachers taking as few as 15 to 20% of the lines. This is the case in certain episodes of Mr. Gow's classes (see Chapter 1), in which students take most of the available talk time and direct the content of the discussion. However, instances of this kind of teaching appear only rarely among the sample of two year college teachers.

Other episodes included small-group work, independent work, and individual conferences. Teachers spent about 12.7% of instructional time on small-group work and about 13.9% on independent work. Once again, the variation among teachers is large. One teacher is coded as using 100% frontal teaching during our observations, whereas another is coded as using only 46.7%. One teacher used small-group instruction 27.9% of the observed time, but four teachers did not use it at all. Five teachers used no independent seat work, but one teacher used it 52% of the time. These are important differences because they help determine the kinds of knowledge in classrooms. For example, when the teacher is talking most of the time, the knowledge is certain to be declarative. The teacher is in the process of announcing what students presumably should learn. The assumption is that if students hear it, they should be able to learn it and act on it. However, we have considerable research demonstrating that such instruction has little effect on learning, especially in writing (Hillocks, 1986) and literature (Nystrand et al., 1997).

WHAT IS THE NATURE AND VARIATION
OF KNOWLEDGE TAUGHT?

We were able to classify the knowledge appearing in our observed classrooms by type of course content and mode of student participation. Type of course content includes substantive, formal-rhetorical, mechanical-syntactical knowledge, and a combination of the latter two. Mode of student participation includes declarative knowledge, to which students listen, but engage in no other observable activity, and procedural knowledge, which requires engagement in observable activity as the instruction proceeds. In addition, we coded a category called explanations of procedures, the kind of knowledge we have seen in Professor James's classes. Conceptually, the explanation of procedures mode is a subset of declarative knowledge, but for purposes of the quantitative analysis, we treat it as a separate category.

Type of Knowledge

For the 19 teachers, the types of content knowledge are distributed fairly evenly, with 21.8% of instructional time devoted to substantive knowledge, 27.7% to mechanics-syntax, 30.6% to formal-rhetorical, and 19.9% to a combination of the latter two (see Table 3.1). At the same time, it is clear that vast dissimilarities exist among teachers. Every range begins at zero and goes to a high of at least 20%, with declarative knowledge related to substance ranging from zero to more than 65%. Some teachers spend no time explaining mechanics, whereas one spends over 40%. Some spend no time on formal-rhetorical knowledge, whereas others spend very large amounts of time on this type of knowledge. In short, the ranges indicate that course content varies considerably from one teacher to another.

Mode of Knowledge

One might expect that courses in writing, those in which a premium must be placed on learning *how* to develop a good piece of writing, would involve primarily learning the procedures for producing effective writing. However, among this group

Table 3.1. Mean Percentage of Observed Instructional Time by Mode and Type of Knowledge

Type of Knowledge	Mode of Knowledge			
	Declarative Knowledge	Explanation of Procedures	Procedural Knowledge	Total
Substantive	11.6 (0-65.8)	5.4 (0-28.6)	4.8 (0-31.0)	21.8
Mechanical-syntactic	6.2 (0-20.1)	13.1 (0-42.5)	8.4 (0-31.3)	27.7
Formal-rhetorical	9.5 (0-37.5)	14.5 (0-40.5)	6.6 (0-31.4)	30.6
Combination mechanical & formal	4.3 (0-34.8)	6.2 (0-25.2)	9.4 (0-32.5)	19.9
Total	31.6	39.2	29.2	100

Notes: Values in parentheses are ranges. Declarative knowledge percentages do not include explanations of procedures; however, such explanations should be considered a special type of declarative knowledge.

of teachers, procedural knowledge appears less than 30% of the instructional time. When it does appear, over half of it is devoted to correcting mechanics in exercises or to editing for mechanics and larger rhetorical-formal issues (e.g., the proper use of topic sentences), not to generating ideas or even to the generation of rhetorical forms. In fact, teachers devote less than 5% of their instructional time to procedures for developing ideas for writing.

During the 2 years of observation, teachers devoted more than 70% of observed class instructional time to the delivery of declarative knowledge. During these episodes, teachers had 89% of the lines of transcript, indicating that students were not engaged in procedures, but were simply listening to what teachers said. In interviews, teachers sometimes referred to these episodes as discussions. When we looked at the transcripts, however, we would find virtually no student response. The term *discussion* seemed to indicate interchanges between teacher and students, but in the event, such expressions often appeared to be metaphors for the sense of *discussion* in which a listener engages simply by listening.

These averages stand in strong contrast to Mr. Gow's numbers, who, as we saw in Chapter 1, devotes the lion's share of time to procedural knowledge related to the analysis of substance. Most teachers in the sample see little need for students to engage in the kinds of tasks involved in developing the content for their various assignments. They believe that explaining the characteristics of the writing (in terms of formal characteristics and conventions) will suffice.

WHAT FACTORS MAY ACCOUNT FOR DIFFERENCES AMONG TEACHERS?

The preceding discussion has emphasized averages for the group of community college teachers, and averages may hide great differences. For example, though class length is mandated, the amount of instructional time afforded students varies widely from one teacher to the next, from a low of 58.5% to a high of 94%. Whereas one teacher devotes all observed instructional time to declarative knowledge, another devotes only 35% to it and the remainder to procedural knowledge. Several teachers spend no observed instructional time on mechanics and syntax, whereas two do little else. Two teachers spend slightly over 60% of instructional time on substantive knowledge, and several spend none. Whereas some teachers only lecture, others devote substantial time to collaborative group work.

Visualize the differences in classrooms that these numbers represent, differences that even a relatively casual observer is likely to notice. In classrooms with little frontal teaching and little declarative knowledge, the teacher will be less the focus of talk. Students will be working in small collaborative groups more often. In teacher-led discussions (TLD), student ideas will be the focus of attention. The teacher will be less a giver of knowledge about writing and more an organizer of an environment that enables students to construct knowledge about writing for themselves.

What are the possible causes of such variations? One may have to do with risk for the teacher. If I hand out the knowledge to be learned, I can hold my students responsible for that knowledge in very specific ways. They either can identify Geoffrey of Monmouth, the Venerable Bede, and the antecedents of *The Wife of Bath's Tale*, or they cannot. But if I am to teach how to write effective essays on topics or with points of view I have not even considered, and if I believe that precise rules for writing such an essay (e.g., the five-paragraph theme[1]) are inappropriate, then I cannot simply lecture on topics and form and be done with it. I necessarily stand on much less solid ground. If I assume that what students learn is in part dependent on what they bring to the learning, how the class members interact, how well I am able to manage those sometimes evanescent interactions, and other open-ended processes, then I cannot control classroom events in the way I can control a lecture.

Several studies have shown that teachers would prefer to avoid the tensions that necessarily arise when information cannot be precisely packaged in lectures or worksheets (e.g., Cuban, 1988; McNeil, 1986; Kahn, 1994). As a result they teach "defensively," in such a way that they gain maximum control over classroom events. They adopt classroom strategies that allow them to retain close control of the content and direction of student response. They adopt policies of testing that focus on recall of specific information, rather than on inference making and more open-ended responses involving interpretation and synthesis. Sometimes they appear to strike bargains with their students, requesting good behavior in return for making the course easy: "All you have to do to pass this class is listen to what I have to say and remember it on tests." Such teaching has been classified as defensive in nature, designed to provide maximum control.

These studies classify other teachers as "adventuresome," willing to make classrooms more student centered and responsive to student needs. Such teachers value student ideas and encourage inference making, problem solving, and creative syntheses. Their classroom processes include teacher-led and small-group student-led discussions that focus on open-ended questions to which the answers are not highly predictable. Their assessments call for inferences and syntheses, perhaps written as essays or developed as creative responses (Smagorinsky & Coppock, 1994) and are what Darling-Hammond, Ancess, and Falk (1995) would call authentic assessments.

Although this interpretation provides some insight into the wide range of variation among our sample of teachers, it cannot account for why the differences exist. It provides an interpretation of the differences, but what factors can account for them? One of the major factors responsible for the differences appears to be teachers' attitudes and beliefs about students.

TEACHER ATTITUDES AND BELIEFS ABOUT STUDENTS

In conducting interviews and later in examining the transcripts, I realized that some teachers made quite optimistic statements about their students' abilities, whereas others made statements that did not display such optimism. It occurred to me that, in some cases, nonoptimistic statements seemed to be linked with high levels of declarative knowledge, high levels of frontal teaching, and what appeared to be simplification of subject matter.

When I began to comb the interview data for signs of attitudes about students, I realized that some teachers made no direct statements about their students' intelligence or abilities to learn. It was, therefore, necessary to decide what other statements might count as indications of such attitudes. Suggestions that students could make contributions to their own learning in various ways and attempts to understand and make allowances for the special circumstances of the students seemed to reflect an underlying optimism. Statements to the effect that students could not be expected to do much on their own, frequently accompanied by lists of student deficiencies, appeared to mark a lack of optimism about their abilities to learn.

Having discussed these assumptions, a research assistant and I attempted to classify teachers as essentially optimistic, not optimistic, or noncommittal, using the major opening interview, one class transcription, and observer notes. Working independently, we agreed on the classification of 16 of the 19 teachers and resolved the remaining 3 in discussion: In all, 13 were classified as essentially optimistic and 6 as nonoptimistic. The cases that follow indicate the range of responses within these categories.

Nonoptimistic

One male teacher who usually teaches English 101, in speaking of errors in student writing says, "I got tired, so sick and tired of seeing so many faults along that line. I wanted to see if I could do a better job in that regard and maybe cut down on some of those faulty expressions in their writing." Asked if it worked, he responds, "I can't say that it has, but I'm not sure that I can say that it hasn't." He comments on the difficulty of working with students who have what he calls "severe . . . deficiencies. . . . people that are perhaps reading and writing at less than eighth-grade level as opposed to somebody that may be at the eleventh- or twelfth-grade level." He continues,

> It seems to me, and again, I may be so wrong, but just from my own personal experience . . . that many of our students have reached the point where the only thing, maybe not the only thing, but they would find most helpful if they had a one-on-one situation.

Another male teacher says this of his students:

> They don't know the rules. They don't know, they don't know words.
> Whatever, it's so oral. . . . a lot of our students come from a very limited
> tunnel-visioned oral language that's spoken in the home. And the written
> language doesn't really have much place in the house, so anything that
> sounds like something else is just automatically the same word. So you get
> *are* for *our*, and you know, you get strange endings on words.

He comments as follows on the thinking of his students:

> I find that they don't think a lot about other than everyday things, and they
> don't think a lot about it in relation to just bringing together ideas or
> finding new ways of looking at things, or bringing in new, bringing in
> information that they have even, but they just don't apply it. And I think
> you see the ultralimited sense of that when you see them write. And that's
> where it becomes its worst.

Two instructors, both teaching English 100, the final remedial class before
English 101, believed strongly that their students had so many problems with
mechanics and usage that their first responsibility was to eliminate those problems. They had a tendency to view dialect differences as "basic" deficiencies that
are very difficult for speakers of nonstandard English to overcome, rather than
differences that result from different circumstances of language learning. These
interviews were never directly pejorative, but they focused on "problems" and
"weaknesses," in great detail without speaking to any strengths of the students.

In addition, we considered various other comments as signs of nonoptimism:
comments about students' inabilities to think problems through beyond the obvious, comments in class to students about their failures to follow directions, to use
appropriate content or form, or to make inferences. Each teacher classified as not
optimistic displayed several of these signs.

Optimistic

Teachers categorized as having a basically optimistic view often made direct
positive statements about their students. For example, one teacher explained that
he ordinarily taught 102, and that he had asked for an additional class for over-
time payment and assumed that he would get a 102 section. It turned out, however, that he was assigned to 100, met the class, and then learned that he would
receive no extra pay. He then had the option of keeping the extra course for one
semester and having a reduced load the next or going back to his normal load. He
explains:

No more money. Just less work next semester, it just balances the thing away. . . . So anyhow, I met the students once, and I liked them, genuinely liked them. I had a good time with them the first time we met, and I liked them as people. . . . Maybe I just got a good group this semester, I don't know. But I like them and they are doing the work and I'm having fun with them as a matter of fact.

One woman who expresses considerable confidence in the ability of her students to grow says, "I find with my students if I can show them specifically what to do in a concrete procedure for doing it, then they can do it. My classes this semester are the best that I've ever had." The second teacher comments on her classes that she finds to be likable for different reasons:

What's so unusual again is that class is so good. The people in that, that class has an older median age than my other classes, and so . . . they're fun people. And they're coming from their jobs and that sort of thing. . . . They're very serious.

Of her other classes, she says, "Then you have the younger students who are more interested in each other and that sort of thing, and that's kind of fun, really."
She does admit to the frustration of teaching the "98s and 99s," the lower-level remedial classes that she describes as being populated by students with third- and fourth-grade reading levels. As I construe her comments, however, her frustrations derive not so much from the "deficiencies" of her students as from a deep sympathy with their plight.
A male teaching English 100 talks about the need for work on grammar and mechanics, but in contrast to the two teachers just discussed whose orientation we categorized as not optimistic, this teacher indicates that students make important contributions to the class. He says,

I try to motivate them as much as I can to generate as much creative thinking as I can which they are all capable of doing. I find repeatedly that they are all capable of doing that.

Another male, teaching 101, begins with the premise that his students think all the time, like everyone else. When he talks about his students he emphasizes his attempt to build on that propensity:

For instance, that first class concluded with their listing in order the qualities that they find attractive in someone of the other sex. What qualities are they looking for in a mate. And after they did that I said, now you have a very rough outline for a classification paper. . . . I want to reintroduce the things they're already doing in their minds. They're sorting out their socks. We'll talk about that as things they classify.

It is interesting to note this in contrast with other teachers who say their students do not or cannot think.

A female in the sample was teaching all English 98 classes. She, too, appears to recognize the plight of the students and determines to do what she can to help them develop. This includes conceptualizing the course as a stepping-stone to English 100. She says,

> Most of these students read on a level between fourth grade and seventh grade, and probably most of them read at the lower level. . . . At this level, English 98, I concentrate on the paragraph. I feel that if these students can write an effective paragraph, then they can go on to English 100 and begin to extend paragraph writing to the essay. I believe that students write best when they're enthused about their topic, and so normally I try to generate some kind of discussion and some kind of enthusiasm for the topic, you know, before they ever begin to write.

We interpret such statements as an indication of this teacher's faith in her students to have ideas and to become interested in others. She plans to build on what they know.

Another woman uses literature as a base for writing in 101. She recognizes that some students are slower to learn than others, yet statements such as the following reveal her faith that they too will learn as she gives them the appropriate help:

> And it comes down to the ones who get it right the first time are those who are fairly intelligent, who are good students already, who pay attention, who understand the concept of modeling, if you will, what they're supposed to be doing. The others, the ones who cannot give it to me in writing yet, when this assignment comes in, can give it to me verbally. We will have talked about it enough that they know, they just don't understand that that's what they're supposed to do on paper yet.

Other teachers whom I call optimistic make similar statements.

EXPLANATIONS AND SUMMARY OF CATEGORIZATIONS

The two categories of optimism and nonoptimism had 13 and 6 members respectively. Five of the nonoptimistic teachers are male and only one is female. Of the

13 optimistic teachers, 5 are male and 8 female. This is a small sample, of course, and it is not appropriate to generalize about gender and attitude much beyond it. It is clear, however, that in this sample, more female than male teachers are optimistic about their students. Interestingly, the four African American teachers share this division with the White teachers, with two females categorized as optimistic and the males as nonoptimistic.

One might expect that the difference in attitude might be related to the racial and ethnic constituencies of the various campuses. The campuses differ sharply in the ethnic and racial makeup of their students. Two are attended almost exclusively by African American (AA) students. Three may be characterized as having predominantly White (PW) student populations, though none is White only. Finally, two may be characterized as racially and ethnically mixed (REM), one of these having high proportions of nonnative speakers of English.

One might expect that optimistic and nonoptimistic attitudes might be related to racial biases of the teachers and the race of students they teach. That appears not to be the case, however. At predominantly AA campuses, optimistic teachers outnumber the nonoptimistic five to two; at REM campuses, five to two; and at PW campuses, three to two. Optimistic male teachers appear in both AA and REM mixed campuses. (See Table 3.2 for a more precise summary of this distribution.)

We might expect that differences in attitude would be related to the course level taught by the teachers. Some of the courses taught by this sample of teachers are remedial and not for credit (English 98 and 100), yet must be taken if students fail to reach a certain level on entrance examinations. Only after passing English 100 are these students eligible to enroll in English 101, a course that must

Table 3.2. Distribution of Teachers Categorized as Optimistic or Nonoptimistic by Campus Ethnicity, Course Level, and Gender (number of teachers)

	Optimistic		Nonoptimistic	
	Male	*Female*	*Male*	*Female*
Campus ethnicity				
African American	3	2	2	0
Racially and ethnically mixed	2	3	1	1
Predominantly White	0	3	2	0
Total	5	8	5	1
Course level				
101	3	6	3	1
100	2	2	2	0
98	0	1	0	0
Total	5	9	5	1

Note: One female teacher counted under course level 100 is also counted under course level 101, as she indicated teaching both levels and being optimistic about both.

be taken and passed for graduation. There is general agreement that the weakest students go to English 98, those testing below seventh-grade level in reading. The students who score well on the entrance exam go to English 101. The course level does not appear to determine attitudes, however. At each course level there are more optimistic than nonoptimistic teachers. Of the six categorized as nonoptimistic, four teach 101 and two teach 100. (Table 3.2 is a summary of these results by gender.)

TEACHING AND ATTITUDES TOWARD STUDENTS

What is the relationship of these attitudes to the way teachers conduct classrooms? The first dimension of our coding had to do with how much time was spent on instruction, management, assessment, and diversion. When we examine the distributions for optimistic and nonoptimistic teachers, we find that optimistic teachers spend about 14% more observed time on instruction than do the nonoptimistic. Over the course of a semester, this would amount to a difference of nearly 7 hours, or 2 weeks, of instruction. Although these differences are not statistically significant, most teachers will recognize how much can be accomplished in 7 hours. It may be that the optimistic are more willing to put in the time involved, certainly a personal decision. (Table 3.3 is a summary of this distribution.)

We also coded the kinds of activities or teacher-student relationships in the classrooms. We categorized these as frontal teaching (in which the teacher controls the class through lecture, recitation, and discussion), conferences, small-group work, and independent work. Since conferences took place so infrequently during our observations, they have been eliminated from the analysis. The differences between optimistic and nonoptimistic teachers in terms of these activities seem no less than remarkable. They are summarized in Table 3.4. Whereas nonoptimistic teachers spend 90% of observed instructional time in lecture and recitation, optimistic teachers spend almost 25% less. This represents a palpable difference. Group work is two and a half times greater in the classes of optimistic teachers than in those of less sanguine teachers. Working independently is more than four and a half times as likely in the classes of optimistic teachers than it is in the classes of

Table 3.3. Proportion of Time in Major Categories of Classroom Time by Attitude Toward Students (percent of instructional time)

	Instruction	Management	Assessment	Diversion
Optimistic	86.6	7.9	2.8	2.5
Nonoptimistic	72.4	13.3	8.0	6.3
All	79.6	10.6	5.4	4.4

Table 3.4. Format by Attitude (percent of instructional time)

	Frontal Teaching	Small Group Work	Independent Work
Optimistic	66.3	15.4	18.3
Nonoptimistic	90.0	6.2	3.9

Note: A chi-square test indicates that the difference between the distributions is statistically significant, $p < .01$.

those who express many misgivings about their students' abilities. We would notice these differences without benefit of statistics.

The differences in time spent on frontal teaching, about 25%, and group work, nearly 250%, would not only feel different in the classrooms, they are statistically significant. In a sense, these results are not surprising. If we believe that our students are very weak, we may very likely believe that they need our direct help at all times. Indeed, several teachers expressed, in one way or another, the need for their students to have direct teacher guidance.

ATTITUDE AND TYPE OF KNOWLEDGE

The differences between optimistic and nonoptimistic teachers by observed types of knowledge are also quite remarkable; see Table 3.5 for a summary. Optimistic teachers spend over 50% more time on the substance of writing than do nonoptimistic teachers. At the same time, they devote far more time to matters of formal characteristics and to combinations of form and syntax-mechanics than do the nonoptimistic teachers. On the other hand, nonoptimistic teachers spend more than twice as much time on straightforward syntax-mechanics, 44% versus 20.3%. Activities coded as focusing on mechanics or syntax almost exclusively involve set exercises to which students must respond. In activities involving a combination of mechanics and formal problems, students almost exclusively respond to

Table 3.5. Attitude by Type of Knowledge (percent of instructional time)

	Type of Knowledge			
	Substantive	Mechanical-Syntactic	Formal-Rhetorical	Combination Mechanical & Formal
Optimistic	24.8	20.3	31.2	23.3
Nonoptimistic	16.3	44.0	26.7	12.7

Note: A chi-square test indicates that the difference between the distributions is statistically significant, $p < .01$.

materials that they or their classmates have written. Each of these differences indicates that the teachers who are more positive are more likely to allow their students greater freedom and responsibility than are their less positive counterparts.

From another perspective, the differences may be the result of different assumptions about the way in which people learn to write. The nonoptimistic appear to believe that the knowledge of writing is hierarchical, that one must know the mechanics of writing and know certain forms of writing before dealing with content. Optimistic teachers, on the other hand, devote 50% more time to content and less than 50% as much time to mechanics. A very old theory of learning to write seems to be at work here, the building-block theory, which holds that before students can proceed to writing paragraphs, they must know how to write sentences; before they can write whole compositions, they must be able to write paragraphs; and so on. I remember one high school English chair who proudly presented his new approach to composition: In ninth grade, focus on the sentence; in tenth, the paragraph; in eleventh, the 500-word theme; and in twelfth, the 1,000-word theme. Today, theorists have largely rejected such a progression. But it has become part of the culture of teaching writing and dies a very slow death.

ATTITUDE AND MODE OF KNOWLEDGE

The distributions of knowledge by mode (student participation) for optimistic and nonoptimistic teachers are presented in Table 3.6. The main difference is that procedural knowledge for optimistic teachers is nearly twice that of the nonoptimistic teachers. This suggests that the more teachers believe that their students can learn, the more willing they are to engage them in the necessary procedures. The less faith they have, the more likely they are to tell them what to do.

Perhaps even more interesting is the distribution of types of knowledge by mode and attitude, which is summarized in Table 3.7. Optimistic and nonoptimistic teachers spend approximately the same amount of time providing declarative knowledge across the four types of knowledge: substantive, mechanical and syntactic, formal and rhetorical, and combinations of formal and syntactic-mechanical.

Table 3.6. Attitude by Mode of Knowledge (percent of instructional time)

| | Mode of Knowledge | | |
	Declarative	Explanation of Procedures	Procedural
Optimistic	31.0	35.4	33.3
Nonoptimistic	33.0	47.7	17.2

Notes: A chi-square test indicates that the difference between the distributions is statistically significant, $p < .01$. Declarative knowledge percentages do not include explanations of procedures.

Table 3.7. Attitude by Mode and Type of Knowledge (percent of instructional time)

	Substantive	Type of Knowledge		
		Mechanical-Syntactic	Formal-Rhetorical	Combination Mechanical & Formal
Declarative knowledge				
Optimistic	11.9	5.9	9.7	3.5
Nonoptimistic	11.6	5.6	9.5	6.3
Explanation of procedures				
Optimistic	6.0	8.0	14.4	6.8
Nonoptimistic	4.2	24.1	14.6	4.8
Procedural knowledge				
Optimistic	6.9	6.5	6.9	13.0
Nonoptimistic	0.5	12.5	2.6	1.6

Notes: Chi-square tests indicate that the difference between the distributions is not statistically significant for the declarative knowledge mode, but is highly statistically significant for the explanations of procedure ($p < .001$) and for procedural knowledge ($p < .001$). Declarative knowledge percentages do not include explanations of procedure.

These differences are not statistically significant. However, large differences appear for explanations of procedures. The nonoptimistic teachers spend over 24% of instructional time explaining how to form sentences, how to punctuate, and so forth (three times more than do optimistic teachers, who spend 8%). Equally surprising, they spend only slightly more than 17% of their time on procedural knowledge and over two-thirds of that is spent on mechanics and syntax. Optimistic teachers, on the other hand, spend a third of instructional time on procedural knowledge, and less than a quarter of that on mechanics and syntax. In short, teachers who are essentially optimistic about their students' abilities are far more likely to spend time on helping them learn procedures for developing whole pieces of writing than are their nonoptimistic counterparts.

This quantitative analysis has indicated clear differences among this group of teachers. Teachers who are optimistic about their students' prospects for learning teach quite differently from those who are not optimistic. Optimistic teachers spend less time on lecture and recitation (66.3% vs. 90.0%) and nearly 250% more time on collaborative group work. Optimistic teachers distribute instructional time fairly evenly over the types of knowledge: substantive, mechanical-syntactic, formal-rhetorical, and combinations of the latter two. Nonoptimistic teachers, however, devote nearly half of instructional time (44%) to mechanical-syntactic knowledge and far less time to substantive knowledge (16.3%). Optimistic teachers spend nearly twice as much instructional time on procedural knowledge and nearly 14 times as much on procedural knowledge related to substance as do nonoptimistic teachers. All of these differences are statistically significant.

At the same time, we see that most teachers rely heavily upon one of the two types of declarative knowledge. Both of these groups appear to stand in contrast to Mr. Gow, who admittedly teaches in a different environment, but who appears to engage his students in the development of procedural knowledge far more frequently than do any of the teachers in the main sample.

In the next three chapters, I will turn to case studies both to examine the differences here in greater detail and to determine what may underlie other differences.

NOTE

1. "The five-paragraph theme" is a standard format for writing taught in many schools and colleges. It calls for an introductory paragraph that presents a thesis statement (sometimes as the final sentence of the opening paragraph) and sometimes with a preview of the points to be made in the ensuing three paragraphs (as in the Illinois state writing assessment). In the following three paragraphs the writer develops one point each in support of the thesis. The final paragraph concludes with a summary of what has preceded it.

❦ 4 ❦

Knowledge of Students,
Purpose, and Content

IN THE PREVIOUS CHAPTER, we saw evidence of a tendency for teachers who are not optimistic about their students to simplify both their teaching and what is taught by delivering declarative knowledge of mechanics or of genre and for optimistic teachers to focus more on procedural knowledge related to either substance or genre. In this chapter we will look more closely at this difference, especially at the interaction of the types of pedagogical knowledge that involve students, purpose, and content in teachers who are optimistic or pessimistic about the students they teach. For greater contrast, I have chosen teachers who, our data suggest, are primarily lecturers. Although the analysis in Chapter 3 reveals significant differences between groups of teachers categorized as optimistic or nonoptimistic, the sample is too small to allow a quantitative analysis to do much more. We still need to know more about why some teachers focus on form, some on mechanics, and some on other aspects of possible writing curricula.

In this chapter and in the two that follow it, I will turn to case analyses, using observational and interview data, so that one may shed light on the other, in contrasting cases. The goal will be to examine contrasting cases in an attempt to better understand the patterns of thinking that appear to result from attitudes toward students and the purposes and content of instruction. The first pair of cases in this chapter will have a focus on the teaching of discourse or genre, whereas the second will have a focus on providing feedback about writing in the classroom.

TEACHING FORMAL DISCOURSE KNOWLEDGE

Perhaps one of the most common ways of thinking about the freshman or high school writing curriculum is to consider what formal or rhetorical knowledge of discourse students should learn (Berlin, 1984). By formal or rhetorical knowledge of discourse I mean knowledge of the purposes, audience, features, or structure, or a combination of these, of certain types or genres of written discourse as con-

53

ceptualized by teachers and textbooks. For example, many high school and college texts and programs single out descriptive writing for instruction. The instruction is likely to include statements about the purposes of such writing for some audience, its features, perhaps criteria for judging it, and so forth. I consider all such knowledge to be formal discourse knowledge.

Case 1: Professor Rose

Professor Rose has taught at one of the AA campuses for many years. He teaches English 101, the first English course that students take for credit.

Expectations of Students. Perhaps the teacher least optimistic in predicting student success is Professor Rose. He ordinarily teaches English 101 and says that his students are "not used to doing . . . virtually any assignment." He continues, "I'm always surprised at how little the students do know about a given subject or a given approach to writing about something." He says,

> I try to talk about editing last, which gives them some comfort, because that's their weakest area, frankly. Perhaps their second weakest area I emphasize a great deal, however, and that is what I would loosely call reading between the lines, thinking for oneself, thinking, using analogy, being creative.

He speaks of his weakest students as having "so many areas of negative thinking that I can't begin to reach, that no matter what I do, there is only minimal improvement."

Purposes. Professor Rose's grand purpose is to teach composition. A guiding principle involves teaching a structure that his students will be able to use:

> There is a tendency on the part of the students to want to be force-fed. The more structure they have, the more comfortable they are with an assignment, and so I have to try and fight that urge to give them too much structure, what I consider too much structure, more or less force them to begin to work things out themselves.

Before we examine that statement in detail, it will be useful to examine what Professor Rose means by structure and what structure he actually does provide. Professor Rose's third assignment is what he calls a classification and provides an example of the pattern followed in each of his assignments, with the exception of narrative. He lays out a set of three topics from which students may choose. Typical topics include the following:

- What are three dangerous drugs?
- What are three situations where we should not drink and drive?
- What are three jobs for the future?
- Who are three well-known illiterates?
- What are the three main reasons for teenage pregnancy?

Before proceeding to develop ideas for these topics, he explains that they need to choose an audience "relatively small in number who might not know this information already, who could benefit from hearing it from the speaker, the writer." His classes "come up with things like my old high school class, my younger brother, my daughter, things of this nature."

In developing the topic, Professor Rose asks his students to find three categories that do not overlap and "that account for the spectrum of possibilities" within the topic. He comments on students' attempts to develop three nonoverlapping categories:

> They had three answers, but they were not answers that covered the
> spectrum of possibilities. Sometimes the answers overlapped. For ex-
> ample, they might have contraceptive for one answer, birth control for
> another answer, or they might have sex education as one answer, and
> discussion about sex, sexual matters with parents as another answer. I saw
> these as being rather similar. And so we started combining our answers to
> the question, so that we would have three distinct answers and then we
> would challenge the class to think of an answer that wasn't covered by
> those three.

In addition, Professor Rose explains his essay format:

> I do have an essay format which explains what a typical five-paragraph
> paper might include: things that might go in an introduction, . . . the
> body, . . . the conclusion. Their paper has to resemble that in some way.
> And until it does they rewrite it.

Professor Rose's criteria for judging pieces of writing help to clarify the nature of this structure and his purpose. As preparation for each assignment, students must write a cover page, which, he says "is something I have invented. . . . [It] is a sheet that allows them to get an introduction essentially, and a kind of coming attraction for what the paper might actually be about." Among other things, the cover page must include "a lead-in . . . and a central idea. It requires a question and some answers." Particularly, the cover page must include a question such as "What are three causes of teenage pregnancy?" along with three answers. When students have written the papers, they hand the cover page to Professor Rose and read the paper

to the class. Frequently, for this reading Professor Rose writes some guidelines
for grading on the board, "so that," he says to one class, "you have a sense of where
we're going." After telling students that he thinks everything has been made clear,
but if they have questions they should ask, he writes a schedule on the board for
the next three meetings along with the following guidelines for grading the stories that some students will read aloud:

THEME 2 (NAR.)

1. Tell story in detail
2. Use appropriate lang.
3. Discuss story's meaning

3 done well = A
3 done effectively = B
1 missing = C
2 missing = D

These indicate that if the paper has all three parts and is done well, it will receive
an A. If the discussion of meaning or the story itself is missing, the paper will
receive a B, and so forth. When asked about the guidelines, he says they are intended as general guidelines to be fair to the students. Professor Rose does not
specify what a story told in detail or what the discussion of the story's meaning
will look like if they are "done well," or "effectively."

We can begin to specify Professor Rose's purposes in teaching composition.
With the exception of the narrative piece, he has narrowed the range of writing to
the "five-paragraph theme," common in high schools and in some colleges, and
simplified the content to three responses to a set question. The only requirement
for the development of content is that the answers not overlap. The responses to
the set question need not be highly developed, in fact cannot be, since the audience chosen is naive. Criteria for evaluating the compositions are loose, focusing
on the readily identifiable presence or absence of substantive parts, suggesting
that students need only supply a token of the part. There is no requirement that
the relationship between the parts be explicated or argued. For example, in writing about three ways to prevent teenage pregnancy, the concern is with finding
categories that do not overlap, not with providing a critical analysis of the possible prevention measures.

In short, the purpose of Professor Rose's teaching is that students learn what
amounts to a formula that may be fulfilled almost algorithmically but that he believes will help them fulfill the demands of writing in college. He has reduced the
task to the simplest kind of school writing and then simplified it further in the
tripartite assignment that calls for loosely related content that may remain highly
speculative because it need not be argued.

Content. To examine the content of instruction, we need to examine both the larger curricular vision of the course and the microcurriculum of the everyday teaching. Professor Rose's curricular vision is based on his view of the "various modes of expository writing." He says, "Most of the courses, I think we probably deal with things like cause and effect, comparison, classification. I do a lot of teaching of use of example as a means of being concrete and getting a point across." Argument he saves for the end of the course, "the last 2½ weeks," as "a kind of preparation for English 102." Some readers will recognize that Professor Rose's course is based on the tenets of what in the field is called "current traditional rhetoric." This brand of rhetorical thinking dates from the 18th-century Scottish commonsense realists, was transformed in the 19th century, and has come to deal generally with expository writing of various types (see Berlin, 1984; Connors, 1981). This rhetoric holds that any topic treated as expository need only explain the "facts" of the case, as though no debate is relevant. Thus, when we present a classification, it is a matter-of-fact presentation, as though the categories established are not open to argument. Such an assumption, of course, simplifies the writing tasks involved.

The content of a writing course of the kind we have here is a perennial problem; students have to write about *something* for each kind of writing covered, and teachers are constantly searching for topics about which students will have enough knowledge to develop an essay. At the beginning of the course, Professor Rose handles that problem by asking students to suggest "about 30 topics per class." He claims that the students brainstorm these topics "for 2 or 3 days in any way that they can from the list of suggestions that I make." A bit later he explains that "after maybe one or two sessions" they vote on the 10 topics that they prefer, "and those 10 become the topics for that class for the semester." Other than "risqué" topics, he says, he accepts any "that I think might bring forth a paper using one of the various expository modes that we're challenged to use, anything from definition to analogy."

Unfortunately, the extent to which students contribute to the set of possible topics is unclear. Certainly, after this initial search for agreeable topics, Professor Rose controls the topics allowed for an assignment. But in each assignment the students choose among three possible options, each of which names the content and sets the parts that must be included.

Professor Rose sets out to teach the expository modes by providing topics and talking about the kind of "things they might come up with." He described to me how he taught what he calls "classification with examples":

PROFESSOR ROSE: OK, well, it turns out that the first paper we wrote, the one that I was using as a model (for papers to follow), tended to be a kind of classification with examples. I wasn't terribly concerned with calling it classification and examples, but because on my cover page I

asked students to write the expository mode they are using, out of
necessity I just gave in to that, which forced me then to talk a little bit
about what classification really means. And so I spent some time
trying to get them to see that a classification is a breakdown of any
subject into its equal parts covering all of its possibilities. . . . And
they were asked to classify all kinds of things. Beginning with the
classroom in terms of everybody in there being a male or female, this
kind of thing. So comfortable with the notion that they had some
sense of what classification is, which later I found out I was wrong,
not everybody did understand that—

HILLOCKS: Was this, was that discussion pretty much, or lecture?

PROFESSOR ROSE: It was discussion, where I would give examples and ask
them to give examples. I would explain how my examples fit and ask
them to explain how theirs fit. We then moved towards developing
questions which would allow for classification based . . . topics.

This is after I had done one on the board. . . . I did a paper on
health on the board, and my question had to do with why. . . . We
never used why, but it had to do with why some club tennis players
lose matches that they should win. And of course it boiled down to
being out of shape. Various scheduling problems, so forth and so on,
in terms of professional people who play in clubs in the evening, and
I told them I had chosen this because what smart students do is they
take some aspect of the subject that they are comfortable with, and I
talked about how most of the PhDs I've known have been working
on one essential thing their whole career, and so you become expert
at something. And I wanted them . . . to write from strength, that's
one of my favorite phrases, and so since I play tennis virtually every
day, I was writing from strength. And so I did a paper, I did a cover
page on health as a topic, . . . with the question and the answers,
showing them how they couldn't possibly think of a reason for a
tennis player not playing well that I hadn't covered in my three
answers, which made mine a legitimate classification. I passed out a
paper on—

HILLOCKS: I'm not sure I understood that. They couldn't think of a
question that—

PROFESSOR ROSE: No, they couldn't think of an answer. They had a
question, I had given them a question on the board. And I had written
three answers on the board. The question had to do with something
about why tennis players don't play up to capacity. Something to do
with the aging process, the scheduling, dissipating habits and so
forth. Family responsibilities. Just mainly the aging process. And I
challenged them to think of an answer to the question which was not

covered by my three general categories. They couldn't do that. I said if you have a question and three answers and I cannot think of a major exception, then I would accept yours as a classification. Then I gave them a paper that I had written years ago, . . . on the ingredients of a happy marriage, and told them that this was a classification and challenged them to think of an ingredient of a happy marriage that I had not included in this paper. And they couldn't. I said, then you should accept this as a classification, and that's the test you should use for your own papers.

It is interesting to note that the essay about a happy marriage is a classic five-paragraph theme that presents the three ingredients (maturity, mutual respect, and economic stability) that he has selected in the opening paragraph and summarizes in the final paragraph. Most of Professor Rose's examples, however, remain rather abstract descriptions of the kind of writing in question. The essay about tennis playing that he "did on the board" is a cover sheet exhibiting what he expects from students. Another example of abstract description, cued by a student's question, appears in the following excerpt from an episode focused on the narrative assignment outlined above:

STUDENT: In the introduction, [are] you supposed to set up the setting, the date and happening, and you know, like who's the character?
PROFESSOR ROSE: I have said repeatedly that is one way of doing it. . . . But it certainly doesn't have to be done that way. You can begin the story with the story itself, which is the way most stories begin. You can if you want to give us some sense of where it is. We need to know something of the background. Last night (refers to previous class) a gentleman told us a story about a guy who was caught in the melee of a fight in some small town the night before a football game. He never told us his relationship to that guy. . . . You know, you've got to identify people for us to identify with them. Just think about the stories you've seen. We always know something about the hero before he gets in trouble, so that we can feel something for him. Clint Eastwood kills 50 people a movie. We don't care anything about it because we don't get to know them. But if something happens to Clint Eastwood, you're very upset. Because at the very beginning of the film you started seeing him. He's got a wife, he's got a home, he's got a car, he's got a job. Personality, a voice. He dresses a certain way, he talks a certain way. You get to know a character. Then you feel something if something happens to that character. But if you don't know anything about a character, just shot him off a roof, OK, that's another dead body. . . . You only care about the

people you have some knowledge of, some identification with. Some reason to think that they were unjustly treated. It was a sad thing that happened to them. . . . (He begins to call role and continues the monologue as he does so.)

This passage of the transcript is typical of Professor Rose's focused classroom talk about discourse. In this episode, he talks about certain abstract characteristics of narrative and what kind of content to include. But he never makes specific recommendations about what procedures to use in developing the narratives or the content.

Case 2: Professor James

Professor James teaches at one of the REM campuses where, like Professor Rose, he teaches English 101. Like Professor Rose, he teaches primarily through lecture. At the same time he exhibits a number of contrasts to Professor Rose's style.

Expectations of Students. Professor James expresses very positive attitudes toward his students. He recognizes the problems that they have, but his basic optimism is indicated throughout the interviews. He praises student writing as he comments on students' response to his suggestion that they write for eighth graders, an audience to which they can write successfully, on a topic for which he requires library research. (Professor Rose would approve of such an audience, but his students need do no research and, therefore, do not have the challenge of translating language and concepts into language that eighth-grade readers will understand.) "A lot of kids," says James,

> did a great job in directing that AIDS essay to the eighth graders. They got rid of a lot of the technical stuff I would have seen in a previous semester and they started to talk to these kids as if these kids could really learn from what they were saying, could avoid casual sex or the demands that their bodies are into at that particular moment. . . . I think that was a highly successful choice of an audience for a number of the students, and I'm going to kind of play with that a little bit as the semester progresses.

His decision to "play" with ideas for audiences to whom his students can write suggests a belief that what he does in the classroom makes a difference in the performance of his students. Therefore, he is eager to "play around," to experiment with shifting the audience to determine what improvements the changes may bring. The change was based on Professor James's desire to get "rid of the technical stuff" and help his students "talk" to the audience, a major tenet of rhetorical theory.

He comments on the dialect that his students bring to class and talks about how he has moved away from "my total allegiance to the students' right to their own language"[1] and come to the point where "we're dealing with survival politics with language skills, with mastery of the formal written dialect, and I teach the formal written dialect as a survival skill. . . . If they make too many errors, it will kill them." He goes on to explain how certain features of West African languages (e.g., noun signifiers that make plural forms redundant) interfere with the use of standard edited English forms. These efforts to understand the students' language and background constitute evidence of positive attitudes, simply by way of contrast to teachers who see nonstandard dialect as evidence of ignorance or stupidity.

He talks about how he continues to revise his course and assignments and makes use of the writing of former students as models of what is possible. For example, he explains that he used to assign Jonathan Swift's *Modest Proposal* and ask students to "write something in a modest-proposal format." He claims that no one ever did that really well. "It was a bad assignment," he says. Students had a hard time reading it and appreciating the point of the satire. He continues,

> So what I've done is come up with a multioption assignment, again, written for a particular audiences. They can, I don't give them Swift's essay unless they choose option one, which is to write a modest proposal but I also give them two other examples of a modest proposal. One was a great essay a student of mine wrote called "Fly the Friendly Skies" in which we could solve airport hijacking by having everyone fly naked. It would eliminate boring in-flight movies. It was a great essay, and it really put a focus on poor airport security and how this would solve the problem because we wouldn't have any place to hide weapons, and the kid did a great job on it a couple of years ago.

Professor James's decision that his assignment was a bad one and his subsequent revision of it, of course, provide further evidence of his positive attitudes. Other teachers simply attribute failure on assignments to their students.

Purpose. Professor James's purpose is implied in his description of the progression of his course:

> I'm moving up from very personal experiences but without lots of heavy judgment analysis or heavy conceptualizing, to a simple massaging and handling of statistics in a report, a reporting of data, to beginning to look at problems and solutions but in fun formats, in the modest-proposal essay, to an essay that also is still potentially fun but is getting them on a higher level in the Bloomian taxonomy[2] or whoever's, to making judg-

ments. But they're judgments about entertainment events. They have to do comparisons, so they're evaluations based on the comparing of two of the same kind of entertainment. . . . They move from there to a trend-analysis essay. They have to look at a contemporary trend and decide what its causes are. . . . They wind up in their final in-class essay, . . . with the reading of two fairly provocative high-level essays on capital punishment, . . . taking competing views on capital punishment and relating that to their own moral views of whether capital punishment is right or wrong, how their views differ or agree with the two principles in the essay reading. The final exam is an even further higher level activity, they have to make a moral judgment about themselves by reading George Orwell's "Shooting an Elephant" and seeing what they would do in a similar situation to Orwell's had they gone through any experience like that. If they put themselves in Orwell's shoes, would they have shot the elephant as well? I'm trying to move up a scale in development, cognitive development in each one of the assignments. . . . There's a component of moral development too. . . . I'm trying to get them to move out of dualism and then other things in the William Perry[3] taxonomy to a point where they begin to recognize there are differing points of view that have equal value. And I found it to be a fairly successful development within the course.

We might say that Professor James's purpose is to teach writing so that it increasingly involves greater complexity in both thinking and discourse. He moves from fairly simple narrative, with which he believes students are fairly comfortable, to complex argument involving moral choices. Further, Professor James places great emphasis on the analysis of content. For example, in describing the "information report," Professor James says,

What they have to do is one of three possible kinds of information report, a process report . . . telling about something they do well and how they do it, a report where they've gone and done research in the library on AIDS. . . . The third option [is that] they have to talk about a kind of music that they like very much and tell why it's good music, or they have to tell about it to a potentially hostile audience, either an older person or someone else, and a few of them choose that. . . . In any case, the information report is . . . to present information about one of these three topics to a particularized audience.

Each of these options demands that students call on or develop a fairly specialized knowledge. His students cannot simply write spontaneously, without structure, but must think about what the audience knows and does not know and make use of special stores of information.

Content. One distinguishing feature of Professor James's classes is that the writings become progressively more complex. Another is that Professor James concentrates on explaining the strategies students should be using in their analysis of the content about which they write instead of providing abstract examples of the kind of material that students should include. In the selection offered in Chapter 2, for example, he is preparing students for an evaluation piece, which may focus on a film, two television shows, a recording of music, or two poems. For each of these, he asks students for ideas about what to evaluate. He explains the general procedures that the students will have to use to make the evaluation of whatever films they choose. Later in the class, after he has presented the dimensions to be judged and suggested ways to go about judging them, his talk turns to the whole piece of writing:

> I cannot stress enough to you that your evaluations will be successful or not based on whether you use good criteria to judge the entertainment event. If the criteria you come up with are appropriate, and if you provide details relevant to each one of the criteria, then you'll have a good paper. There's no escaping it. A good judgment has got to judge whether it was realistic or whether it was appropriate, be more than simply empty general opinion. I like it, I really like that music. That means it just inspires me, it makes me feel good. Well, you're on the point there. *Why* does it make you feel good? . . . Why does it inspire you? What is it about it? I like the message in the songs. What do you like about the message of the songs? (He provides several more examples of such questions.) You've got to come up with . . . specific reasons why something is good or not good.

Throughout the lecture, Professor James presents specific explanations of procedures (declarative knowledge of questions to ask and answers to find) for conducting this kind of evaluation.

Comparison and Contrast

Although Professors Rose and James differ in their attitudes toward students, they have in common very high levels of frontal or presentational teaching, James at 91% and Rose at 95%. Both also have comparably high levels of focus on knowledge of discourse or genre. They organize their courses around their own versions of "current traditional rhetoric" (Berlin, 1982, 1984), e.g., classification, problem-solution, evaluation, and so forth.

Beneath these ostensible similarities lie some striking differences. In particular, differences show up when we examine the type of knowledge in their classrooms. All of Professor Rose's talk is declarative knowledge about the features or substance of the compositions he wants students to write, knowledge of the formal features of the writing he expects. Professor James, on the other hand, directs his talk to explanations of procedures that students must use to produce the writing, what he calls the "cognitive demands" of the tasks involved. Professor Rose tells students what parts the compositions must have and gives examples of the kind of content that will suffice. Professor James gives students the procedures for developing the content: to evaluate, find appropriate dimensions for judgment, make judgments based on the analysis of particulars, and then support the judgments with particular reasons.

Both of these teachers stand in contrast to Mr. Gow, who focuses on what I have called procedural knowledge by engaging his students in the procedures of interpreting the imagery of the engravings that he uses on the assumption that his students will not learn the procedures well enough to use them on their own unless they engage in using them with some level of support. Mr. Gow would see simply explaining the procedures as inadequate.

Although both Professors Rose and James use versions of current traditional rhetoric as the basis of their curricula, they differ in the way in which they structure the course. Professor Rose begins with a classification paper, moves to narrative, and then returns to classification. He presents the other "modes of expository writing" in a sequence that is fairly arbitrary; at least, he suggests that the order does not matter, with the sole exception of argument, which he saves until the last 2½ weeks of the semester as preparation for English 102. Each of the modes, outside narrative, must have three of something, whether that be categories, causes, reasons, examples, or characteristics. The course is not planned to build from simple to complex or to increase the challenge to the students. It appears to be planned so that students have several opportunities to work on the basic five-paragraph theme.

The evaluation practices of the two teachers also differ in interesting ways. Professor Rose tells his students that the narrative has three components: the story, its discussion, and appropriate language. If all three of these are done well, the paper will receive an A, and so forth. As I have noted, however, he does not explain any of these in detail. Nor does he when he comments on the papers that are read aloud later in the class. It appears that the main criteria for his evaluation have to do with the presence or absence of the parts. In the case of the five-paragraph theme, his concern is whether the introduction, three body paragraphs, and conclusion are present.

Professor James, on the other hand, reveals more explicit and detailed criteria for evaluation. He is primarily concerned with whether students have met what he calls "the cognitive demands" of the task. He conceptualizes them as comparable to the procedures that he outlines. All of this implies that he is far more concerned with the development of content than is Professor Rose, who is concerned primarily with the inclusion of the parts of the essays he has stipulated. To gain greater insight into Professor Rose's criteria for grading, I will turn to a context in which these may be examined more closely.

FEEDBACK ON WRITING

After they have written their essays, Professor Rose calls upon several students to read their narratives to the class. On the board he has written his grading system: "(1) tell story in detail; (2) use appropriate lang.; (3) discuss story's meaning." Horace proceeds to read his story, called "Auto Theft." His car had been stolen by a 15-year-old boy with a long criminal record. At the conclusion of the reading, Professor Rose speaks:

> PROFESSOR ROSE: What all is the meaning of that? What does the story mean? What's the point of it?
> HORACE: Auto theft, and it's not necessary to look at the older people for the auto theft, it could be children.
> PROFESSOR ROSE: Anybody else get anything, anybody get anything else from that story? I want you to write out some possible meaning for that story you've written.
> (Horace mutters inaudibly.)
> PROFESSOR ROSE: Anybody get [public radio]? This morning on public radio I heard a judge from Wisconsin discussing crime, and he cited a study which indicates that there is a direct correlation between the swiftness of punishment and the absence of repeating crime. This boy was 15 and had 16 offenses already. Two years in [an institution for boys] after your 16th offense doesn't sound like very much. [That institution] is not a jail, of course. It's a school for boys, some of whom are so-called (inaudible), some of whom come from broken homes.

After 30 lines of talk about the culprit and his punishment, Professor Rose continues his advice:

> PROFESSOR ROSE: The reason why I'm doing this is because I want Horace to hear some suggestions. I want you to write out a more meaningful interpretation of that story, I think there's more to it than just a boy stealing a, taking a car for a joyride, getting a couple of years in [the institution]. Think about, for example, what kind of life he must have had to have committed 16 crimes in 15 years. He obviously started early.
> HORACE: Right, so—
> PROFESSOR ROSE: What does that mean in terms of his future, I wonder. What's being done to rehabilitate him, why do you suppose he had done all this in the first place, and what are we doing to encourage him, by giving him such meaningless punishment. Those are the kinds of things I want you to think about.
> HORACE: All right.

It is interesting to note that although this teacher's orientation is to generalized discourse knowledge (in this case, story plus discussion), his way of explaining how to fulfill the discussion part is to suggest what the student might have said. He uses a comparable technique when he assigns the next piece of writing, one that "demands the use of examples." He expounds on several possibilities for developing the topics. Bereiter and Scardamalia (1987) call this *substantive facilitation*. He tells the students in each case what kinds of things to include in their essays. In effect, he does the work for the students. If he were to use what Bereiter and Scardamalia call *procedural facilitation*, he would help students learn procedures for interpreting their own stories.

It will be useful to compare Professor Rose's feedback after reading aloud with that of another professor. Professor Thomas has spent time as a professional journalist. She spends as much time on frontal teaching as does Professor Rose. As a means of showing her students what is involved in revising, she presents a lecture that runs 225 lines of transcript for the teacher, with 7 for the students. It certainly involves declarative knowledge. However, to encourage her students to think about revision, she begins her lecture on the kinds of things writers do when they revise and passes around her first draft of a story that was published in a large metropolitan newspaper, a story about a trip she had taken on a new road that went above the Arctic Circle. She explains how she collected notes and wrote a draft that contained far more than she needed for her 1,000 word story, asks students to look for changes in her handwritten manuscript, which is traveling around the room, and indicates that she did a total of six drafts before she had the final story. Following this lecture, she asks to hear a student's draft:

PROFESSOR THOMAS: I'm really anxious to hear your drafts at this stage of the game. . . . Sounds like you've worked hard to get to this stage. Now. Remember, . . . one of the things that I want to show you out of this is that no writer that I know can write as well as they possibly can write the first time. So your drafts that we're going to hear, we all understand they're not your best writing. They're a draft. So we're going to listen and act as . . . your audience, . . . as your listeners, as your readers. And Jane, is it OK to start with you?

(Jane indicated earlier that she is having problems.)

JANE: That makes sense.

PROFESSOR THOMAS: All right. Now remember, one of the things we want to listen to in Jane's piece that she needs help with is staying on the topic. So, listen for all the things that you've been working on. (She lists five questions.) Jane, if you could read loudly and slowly, . . . all of us will really listen so that we can give all the help we can.

JANE: I know the caffeine in coffee is bad for me. But the tantalizing aroma of freshly perked coffee sparks a craving I just can't resist. I guess you could say the aroma turns me on. I sense a smell awakening my taste buds and the memory of the last great-tasting cup of coffee I consumed. My sense of smell awakens two of my other senses, taste and memory. The aroma of fresh-baking bread in my oven brings back the memories of my youth. I see my mother busy in her kitchen, putting on the final preparations for Thanksgiving dinner, slicing her homemade bread, basting the huge delicious-smelling turkey, putting whipped topping on the pumpkin pie, but most of all, the warm feeling of love I felt for her washes over me. . . . Our sense of smell can trigger good and bad memories.

Jane's piece moves from here to other smells, the memories they evoke, and then to the sense of sight and a list of things that she likes to see. Her final sentences are,

The sight of an airplane climbing up into the heavens thrills me. I remember the first and only time I flew. (ends reading) That's as far as I go.

Professor Thomas then cues the feedback:

PROFESSOR THOMAS: Mm-hmm. OK. All right, what can we say to Jane about her piece? Is her thesis clear? We're going to start there. Carl?

CARL: I think so. Is the thesis on your senses?

JANE: Yes.

STUDENT: She goes into each one. She's very detailed.

PROFESSOR THOMAS: Hm. Mmhm. Jane, would you read your beginning again please?

JANE: I actually have two or three beginnings, I kept the second one. The first one, I said, I love coffee, but I know that caffeine in it is bad for me. We're not going to need that. I went to, I *know* the caffeine in coffee is bad for me.

PROFESSOR THOMAS: Keep going.

JANE: OK. (reads the first four sentences above).

PROFESSOR THOMAS: Hm. OK. All right. I can see how you're wandering. I mean, it's kind of, I don't know what to say but . . . Anyone, reactions? feedback? (no response) Did this start with an "I love coffee" that came off of your list? (Professor Thomas had asked students to make a list of possible topics.)

JANE: Yeah. No this wasn't on my list, the item of coffee wasn't on my list.

PROFESSOR THOMAS: Oh. That's all right. It would have been—

JANE: How I started it was, I am a coffee freak, I mean I can drink three
pots of coffee a day, but I, it's bad for me. . . . And I walked into my
friend's home and she had coffee perking. Oh God, would I love to
have a cup of that coffee. So I knew I couldn't have it but it drove me
crazy. It's the aroma. And that's how I started.

PROFESSOR THOMAS: OK. Tim?

TIM: I thought the better way to start out was going to be with an exposition of why she loves coffee so much and how she can't [stay away
from it.]

THERESA: You could just write about coffee.

PROFESSOR THOMAS: Yeah, yeah. I can imagine a really fine paper on I
love coffee. Period. You're right about sense of smell is one of our
strongest senses of association. Smelling something will bring back
memories faster than any other sense. . . . One of the things I hear
you saying is, one reason I love coffee is that it brings back wonderful memories to me. . . . And that's a place where you could stick
your Thanksgiving, or other special occasions that come back to you.
That's all, remember your topic sentence. . . . Another reason why I
love coffee is—why else? Just what you said. It's always an occasion
to sit across the kitchen table with a friend and chat.

JANE: Yeah, yeah.

PROFESSOR THOMAS: So then you can talk about that. . . . The whole thing
is why I love coffee. I think at the end you could mention that you
know it's bad . . . that you can't drink as much as you want. But the
focus is on your loving it.

JANE: That's where I got, I just turned off . . . of what I was trying to say
completely. I kept going.

PROFESSOR THOMAS: OK. Do you think that that's more on the track? That
this will help?

JANE: Yeah, probably. I would probably be better off sticking with the I
love coffee and what you say, going down those various reasons
why. . . . The trying to go to the senses is such a vast area that I can't
handle it, and this is what happens.

These two sets of feedback are superficially similar. The students read their
writing and the professors indicate what should be done. A closer look indicates
some striking differences between them. Professor Rose, in essence, tells Horace
what information he might include. Professor Thomas allows a kind of partner-
ship in thinking about the revisions and suggests them much more indirectly,
through student comment and through Jane's own words: "One of the things I
hear you saying is, one reason I love coffee is that it brings back wonderful memo-

ries to me." The result is not a substantive facilitation, but a nudging into procedural knowledge. Her coaching emphasizes what is already strong in Jane's writing and has the effect of helping Jane see it. By the end of the interchange, Jane appears to have appropriated that insight.

CATEGORIES OF TEACHER KNOWLEDGE

With these cases for consideration, having already considered knowledge of students in the preceding chapter, I will return to two other categories of teacher knowledge: purpose and content.

Purposes

In part, Grossman's (1990) statement about purposes assumes that there exists a set of purposes for teaching a subject that can be known by the teachers. We have to ask, What would it mean to know such a body of purposes? Would they include the full range of purposes that have been enunciated for the subject? Or those enunciated in current issues of the relevant subject matter journal for teachers, in this case the *English Journal* or *College Composition and Communication*?

Shulman's (1986, 1987) and Grossman's (1990) statements suggest that the purposes for a subject as a whole are unified. We can think of the purposes of a subject as unified if the level of abstraction is high enough. We could say, for example, that the purpose of all education is to promote the growth of all individuals for active participation in a democracy, one of the ultimate purposes of education in the United States.

But the subject matter teacher does not often ask that question. More often, she asks what curricular experiences will help students become readers of novels, successful users of concepts in geometry, or in our case, better writers. We may think of these purposes as general purposes of the subject matter. Experience suggests that subject matter teachers often reduce these questions to what must be covered in a given course, without examining what it is, other than content, that students will learn. That is, they are concerned that a particular novel be covered, for example, *The Scarlet Letter*, and do not necessarily attend to the question of whether the students are becoming better readers of novels in the process. Coverage, in and of itself, appears to be the goal.

Teachers have purposes that exist at a lower level of abstraction than the general subject matter goals. For example, many use specific activities in conjunction with particular works to improve reading, not simply to cover the material (cf., Wilhelm, 1997). The more specific purposes of these activities, for example, to imagine characters in a novel, may be seen as instrumental in reaching general subject matter goals, for example, to read literature more effectively.

As teachers, then, we appear to think about purposes at three levels of abstraction, at least. We can expect to find considerable agreement at the higher levels of abstraction. In the United States, most teachers would be likely to pay at least lip service to the purpose of enabling their charges to become active participants in a democratic society. We can also expect high levels of agreement among teachers at the level of general subject matter goals. What teacher of English, for example, would not agree to one purpose of English: the appreciation of literature? This high agreement suggests that the purposes at the levels of ultimate and general subject matter goals may be unified and may exist as a general body of purposes to be learned. However, as we have seen, teachers simply do not agree on the best ways of reaching general subject matter goals. The result is widely divergent classroom activities and subject matter content.

Further, it seems apparent that different subject matter and different instrumental goals have different consequences for the more abstract ultimate goals. For example, Professor Rose's goal is for students to learn the five-paragraph theme for writing about topics treated as exposition for naive audiences. As I have already noted, the information conveyed is treated as not debatable so that there is no need to argue points. This subject matter goal reflects an authoritarian stance concerning the nature of discourse, a stance that is acted out in Professor Rose's classroom. Professor James focuses on the "cognitive strategies" that he sees as necessary to arguing a case, indicating the need for discourse to reflect the consideration of other points of view and opinions. In Professor James's class, too, the major activity is listening to what the teacher has to say, an activity that is at odds with the ultimate aim of democratic classrooms. In Mr. Gow's class, on the other hand, students have most of the lines of talk and largely control the direction of the discussions, especially in their small groups. In this instance, the instrumental goal (for students to develop and defend interpretations of Hogarth's engravings) supports both the subject matter goal and the ultimate goal of democratic classrooms.

Where do these purposes, or goals, come from? In these cases, the ultimate purpose concerning democratic classrooms comes from a long tradition in American education. All three of these teachers indicate that they hope to prepare students for life beyond their own classrooms, including life in a democratic society. But they adopt different paths to that goal. In effect, they reconstruct the purpose for themselves. Their subject matter goals are fairly similar, if we discount Professor Rose's exclusion of argument from exposition. However, here again, they have reconstructed these goals in accordance with their views of subject matter, students, and teaching. The specific instrumental goals of Professors Rose and James also have a long history in teacher lore (five-paragraph theme) or textbooks (how to write an evaluation). These, too, have been reconstructed by each professor. Mr. Gow's activity, with its own unique instrumental goal, is an invention, a construction, developed to align with his vision of teaching.

The activity and talk of every teacher in this study can provide considerable evidence of similar reconstruction and construction of purposes. Most purposes at each of the levels are available, and teachers can and do adapt them to their own uses and according to their own interpretations.

Content

By and large, the question of what is appropriate content knowledge for teachers of writing is open to debate and likely to remain so for some time. At the level of freshman college writing and school writing programs, the consensus appears to favor a version of rhetoric that many experts call "current traditional rhetoric." James Berlin (1984) has traced the development of this rhetoric to the Scottish commonsense realists of the 18th century. Early versions of this rhetoric focused on the modes of writing: description, narration, exposition, and persuasion.

High school programs have not moved far from this analysis of writing. Up until very recently, for example, the immensely popular Warriner series published by Harcourt Brace focused on these modes exclusively with emphasis on these types of paragraphs before moving to full compositions, but always reserving persuasion for the 12th grade and the end of the book. In 1993 Holt, Rinehart and Winston, a subsidiary of Harcourt Brace Jovanovich (now Harcourt Brace) published a new edition of Warriner with James L. Kinneavy as editor. For the first time, the series began to include what Kinneavy and others call expressive writing and made use of Kinneavy's ideas of literary purposes in writing (cf. Kinneavy, 1971). However, the 1993 edition of Warriner still includes work on the four modes of writing. Many state mandatory writing assessments are based on a version of current traditional rhetoric. In the Illinois assessment, for example, the writing tasks include narrative, expository, and persuasive. Similar parallels can be shown for many other state writing assessments.

In college writing, things changed. After the beginning of the 20th century, college composition began to focus on a single mode, exposition. Textbooks that focused on exposition dealt with types of exposition: definition, classification, comparison-contrast, examples, cause and effect, evaluation, and so forth (Connors, 1981). This has been the dominant rhetoric of the past 100 years. It is still in common use today in schools and colleges. Innovative, popular freshman texts, such as *The St. Martin's Guide to Writing* by Axelrod and Cooper (1991), still attend to the various types of expository writing.

In this rhetoric, content knowledge for the teaching of writing commonly includes an understanding of these types, or modes, and their features. For example, the Kinneavy Warriner text explains the two methods of organizing the comparison-contrast piece as the "block method" and the "point-by-point method." But it also includes a section on the features that all of these modes of writing have in common: introductions, bodies, conclusions, thesis statements, and so forth.

However, other rhetorical positions will deny the importance of the thesis statement and the divisions of writing into these modes. For example, I have argued that anything we write must be in a sense persuasive, or it will not be effective (Hillocks, 1995). Many scholars argue that exposition is really argument, often complete with claims, grounds, warrants, backing for warrants, and rebuttals that we find in Toulmin's (1958) analysis of argument. Bazerman (1988) has argued that scientific writing is not simply exposition, as many people think, but that it has a long tradition of rhetorical persuasion. The point is that although current traditional rhetoric dominates the teaching of writing in schools and colleges, it is not the only viable rhetorical theory.

Any one textbook necessarily includes only a fraction of the knowledge that is available for teaching a subject, and that fraction will be what the writers and editors believe to be a coherent and teachable fraction of the whole. Likewise, teachers can include only a part of the whole in their classes, that part being filtered through their own interpretations and reconstructed for use with a particular class.

SOME DYNAMICS OF TEACHER KNOWLEDGE

What we see in the cases presented here are striking differences in attitudes toward students, in the instrumental goals set for students, in the differences in content presented, and in the resulting differences in the microcurriculum. These differences suggest that knowledge in any one category does not exist independently of knowledge in other categories. Rather, what a teacher knows in one category is likely to be dynamically related to knowledge in other categories. In these and the following discussions, I do not refer to knowledge as the kind of static statements that one may draw from a textbook, a research report, or an encyclopedia article, but what teachers have in mind as they proceed in their teaching, their selections, interpretations, beliefs, and reconstructions.

Given that definition of knowledge, it is clear that there exists a dynamic relationship between knowledge of students, purposes, and knowledge of discourse and that this dynamic has a powerful impact on what happens in classrooms. If we know a teacher's attitudes toward students, we can predict whether the teacher's instruction will involve simple or complex subject matter or instrumental goals and purposes with their attendant representations of subject matter. When the teachers in this sample are nonoptimistic about their students, we can predict that their instrumental goals will involve far simpler tasks than those of teachers who are optimistic, that their teaching will stress the mechanical and formulaic in discourse and in the substantive that they will settle for the mundane, and that they will allow little opportunity for response and discussion. In one nonoptimistic teacher's class, students' writing amounts to little more than copying and inserting correct punctuation. For other students, assignments are so highly structured that the students have little opportunity to learn more than the simple formula that produces the five-paragraph theme, which has become almost a fill-in-the-blank exercise.

Professor Rose's talk indicates several ways of simplifying writing tasks, and, therefore, the teaching involved. First, directing the piece of writing to an audience that knows little of the topic, even when no specialized knowledge is involved (my younger brother), legitimizes writing from a paucity of information and renders finding additional information unnecessary.

Second, his requiring the tripartite structure reduces complexity. When we deal with causes or characteristics of any phenomenon, we cannot begin by assuming that there are only three or as many as three. To adopt such an overarching rule is to short-circuit and simplify the thinking involved. However, Professor Rose believes that his students will be unable to learn what he hopes they will, even with this structure. But he also believes that "the more structure they have, the more comfortable they are with an assignment."

Third, the tripartite structure sets up the five-paragraph theme, still popular among English teachers even though widely criticized by many (e.g., Emig, 1971) as formulaic and oversimplified. Finally, Professor Rose, in his criteria for judging the writing, is concerned only that the parts be present and "done well," an expression that remains undefined.

Professor James, who has high expectations for his students, does not set the limits imposed by the five-paragraph theme. His assignments grow in complexity in terms of both cognitive and moral considerations. He stipulates an eighth-grade audience for one paper, but it is one that also requires library research, and his intent is that students translate the technical language that they find in their sources to language appropriate for a younger audience. His criteria for grading are tied to a conception of what the task involves. For example, in an evaluation, he expects his students to identify dimensions of what is to be evaluated (in a movie, the acting, the set, photographic angles, and so forth), to examine those dimensions, make judgments about them on the basis of the evidence in the product examined, and develop an evaluation of the whole from their thinking about the individual dimensions. (He does not require three dimensions.) These criteria are both more explicit and more complex than are Professor Rose's.

Although Professor Rose's general subject matter goal is to teach writing, his instrumental purposes have been strongly influenced by his belief that his students are weak and, for their survival, need the restrictive structures that he provides. His purpose is to present a simple set of guidelines for students to follow. These guidelines become a formula that ignores the careful development of content.

In the case of feedback, Professors Rose and Thomas both hope that they will enable students to recognize, rectify, and perhaps avoid problems in their writing in the future. In this, they share similar general subject matter goals. However, Professor Rose conceptualizes his role as one of simply telling students what substantive material they should include in their writing and what mechanical and structural errors they have made. His goal is simply to make his explanations clear. In contrast, Professor Thomas tries to engage students in thinking through problems in their writing so that they themselves will use their own knowledge to identify and consider them. This difference in action represents a major difference in instrumental goals and purposes.

We cannot conclude absolutely that attitudes toward students are the cause of simplifications of purpose and content. However, what teachers themselves say lends credence to that interpretation. It may be, of course, that some teachers began teaching in a simplified way, and when students did not respond with interest, assumed that students were slow and so justified the teachers' simplifications. Another possibility is that these two tendencies may be related to other variables that are somehow responsible for both. Whatever the case, it seems to me there is no doubt that teachers' beliefs about students strongly influence their decisions about the purposes and content of instruction.

NOTES

1. Professor James is referring to a resolution of the Conference on College Composition and Communication that was passed in the 1960s. In essence, it stated that all students have a right to their own language (that is, the dialect that they learned in the process of growing up) and that teachers have no business trying to change it or impose another language on students.

2. Professor James refers to Benjamin S. Bloom, ed., *Taxonomy of Educational Objectives. Handbook I: Cognitive Domain* (New York: David McKay, 1956). This has been an important book in its influence on schools and thinking about curriculum. It provides a taxonomic analysis of intellectual skills and abilities ranging from comprehension to evaluation.

3. Professor James here refers to a study by William G. Perry titled *The Forms of Intellectual and Ethical Development in the College Years: A Scheme* (New York: Holt, Rinehart, and Winston, 1970), which examines the the nature of intellectual and ethical growth from what Perry calls basic dualism (right, wrong; we, they) through increasing awareness of and ability to deal with multiple points of view and frames of reference. Essentially, Professor James's description of the increasing problematics of his course parallels parts of Perry's scheme.

❧ 5 ❧

Substance and Constructivist Teaching

FOR THE THREE TEACHERS described in Chapter 4, lecture-recitation is the dominant mode of instruction, with a focus on discourse knowledge. In this chapter, I will examine substantive knowledge and the teaching of procedural knowledge and how these differ from the declarative knowledge of discourse. The major questions will be the following: What are the assumptions underlying these differences in teaching? What do the differences imply about the underlying views of teaching and learning?

SUBSTANTIVE KNOWLEDGE

Most of the talk about purpose in textbooks on writing has to do with the impact that a piece of writing has on an audience, to have the audience understand, believe, or to do something. At the same time, the authors of these books are usually concerned that the writer have a clear idea of what he or she wants to say. The implication of this concern is that understanding the subject matter of writing is part of the writer's purpose. Professors Rose, James, and Thomas and many others in this sample all reveal a concern with purpose in their assignments, if not in their class work, usually in the sense of making ideas clear to audiences. At the same time, as we saw in Chapter 4, these same teachers tend to concentrate on the students' learning features of written structures such as classification or the five-paragraph theme and do little or nothing with the substance of writing. Teachers in this sample devote only 21.8% of instructional time to substantive knowledge, and when they do, over half the time is lecture or recitation about the substance. They spend 5.4% of instructional time explaining procedures for generating or transforming knowledge. They spend only 4.8% of instructional time engaging students in the procedures for developing content. Instead, most teachers spend large portions of instructional time on abstract features of discourse at the formal or mechanical levels. This policy appears to be based on the assumption that learning the structure or features of something like classification is tantamount to learning how to manipulate the content involved in order to construct a classification. Research on the teaching of writing provides very strong evidence, however, that the two are very different: programs focusing on how to investigate and construct content have an effect several times greater than programs focusing exclusively on learning the features of the structures. These programs are referred to as focusing on inquiry and models, respectively (see Hillocks, 1986).

Every teacher of writing deals, at some level, with the content of writing. When Professor Rose tells Horace what should be included in the discussion of his story, he deals with the content of writing (see Chapter 4). When Professor Thomas helps Jane see problems in her "wandering" through a vast area, she deals with the content of Jane's writing. What I am concerned with here is distinctly different. Some teachers deal not only with the content of writing in some stage of drafting, but with *substance* that is *potential* content, with content prior to the selection of some of it for writing. For example, when teachers lead a class in brainstorming a topic, they are dealing with potential content. When Mr. Gow's class discusses Hogarth's engravings, students are learning strategies for dealing with potential content.

This study indicates that many teachers concentrate their efforts on formal or mechanical discourse knowledge. Far less frequently, teachers make content a primary focus. When they do, it is more often through declarative statements than through engaging students in using the procedures. I will turn first to episodes in which we find declarative knowledge of substance.

Declarative Treatment of Substance

Teachers deal with substance in writing courses for various purposes. Professor Wade talked to his students about the results of his survey concerning what qualities they said they wanted in a mate (see Chapter 1). Presumably, Professor Wade simply wanted students to have an example of the kind of analysis that he hoped they would do in the assignment. Professor Jenkins conducts a class on *Macbeth* in which he plays an audio recording of portions of the text, asks some questions, and explicates parts that he thinks require explanation. After listening to a recording of the sleepwalking scene, Professor Jenkins conducts the following discussion:

> PROFESSOR JENKINS: That's a great scene. So what happened? What did
>   she do? . . . She's what?
> ANDREA: Sleepwalking.
> PROFESSOR JENKINS: She's sleepwalking, and in every sleepwalking
>   [scene] there are people who sleepwalk, and usually it's a sign, or can
>   be, a sign of some emotional unrest and it's a way of kind of working
>   it off, you know, in some odd way. Now for her though, what is she
>   doing? She's doing what?

DARNELL: Acting out the murder.

PROFESSOR JENKINS: She's acting out the murder, reliving the murder again, about Banquo and there being so much blood. Look what she says, now Shakespeare is so, the way he does things, he has her say earlier in the play a little water will clear us of this deed. This is what you can wash hands with, Macbeth. There's nothing to blood. You can wash it off. She says now, all the perfumes of Arabia couldn't sweeten this little hand, you know. So Shakespeare began the thing with one image and uses the very same image later on in the play. Where Macbeth says if I put my hands in the sea it would make the ocean turn all wine red. She said, "No, go to the faucet. Go to the john. Get some water. Wash your hands." You know. But now this is all coming back on her. And psychologically now she is washing her hands. If you've ever seen the thing as a play, you know, you see her kind of wash off the spots of blood on her hand. And the physician, the doctor who is there and the lady who attends her know that . . . , she's revealed what has happened.

In this example the focus is on possible content, not on the features of some composition that students will write. Further, the knowledge involved is declarative. It is delivered by the teacher to the students. Perhaps Professor Jenkins hopes that his explications of the imagery in *Macbeth* will enable students, by example, to explicate imagery for themselves. However, the students are not engaged in developing explications here, as they are in Mr. Gow's class, nor is Professor Jenkins providing instruction in how to do so. He is merely presenting his own explications.

Other examples are not so clear. It is a very common practice of the teachers in this sample to ask students to read their compositions aloud. In Professor Rose's class, as we saw in the previous chapter, when Horace reads aloud, the focus is on the content—what the student has read and the content that Professor Rose suggests ought to be there. In Professor Thomas's class the focus moves from the content of the student piece that is read aloud to consideration of how it can be better focused, to manipulation of the existing writing. If a teacher provides a set of guidelines to use in locating and evaluating discourse features as the composition is read aloud, we coded the episode as focusing on discourse knowledge. If, on the other hand, students are simply asked to listen, then we coded the episode as substantive knowledge.

The following directions make it clear that Professor Rose essentially wants students to listen to the reading while he writes comments on their cover pages:

I want you to come up here and read it from the desk. Or you can stand in front of the room. We're going to suddenly become a public-speaking class. But I'm not going to grade you on those things. I know you won't have poise and confidence. The main thing is just to enjoy telling the story.

Sometimes discussions of issues appear but are structured so that they do not qualify as procedural knowledge. Take one example from a class taught by Professor Carter at an AA campus. He is one of the several male teachers who are not optimistic about the probability of success for his students. Our observations indicate that his dominant mode of instruction is presentational and that most of his class time is devoted to the "forms of discourse" in expository writing, in much the same way as is Professor Rose's. Like most of the teachers who are not optimistic, Professor Carter gives substantive knowledge a low priority. On one occasion it becomes the primary focus of instruction, when he explains to his students that he wants to tell them "a little bit about argumentation. I also want to give you a pretty good idea of what we mean by an argument. It isn't quite the same as what we're accustomed to [thinking]." In response to his question, "What happens in an argument?" one student responds, "People are upset about something," and another says, "They disagree about something." Professor Carter asks the students if they have strong feelings about anything and suggests that some people have strong feelings about eating pork. He says,

> Now you hear a lot of people—people are becoming more and more touchy about their diet. At least they say that they are. Do you have any strong feelings about either that topic or anything else? Maybe you have strong feelings about the upcoming election. Or maybe about a car. Maybe about women (students laugh). Yeah. Fellows?

Finally one student says, "We had a debate one year about whether we were pro or con on gay people." Professor Carter accepts that as "a good hot issue," and asks the students to be "more specific about what the topic was, about gay people." The student says that the debate had been about whether gays should be allowed to work in public places. The remainder of the class is devoted to students' expressing various ideas about gay people, including whether "gay is a race," how gays have sex, whether gay people should be role models, the inappropriateness of "putting gays down," gay people and AIDS, and so forth. Each of these generated various opinions often delivered vociferously and usually in a rush, so that no topic takes more than a minute. The teacher's intent in this episode is simply to let students know that these are the kinds of issues that people develop arguments about and perhaps to let them see how people disagree. We coded it as declarative knowledge of substance.

Substance and Procedural Knowledge

Far less frequently, teachers in our sample engage students in using procedures for manipulating the potential substance for writing. Because this is a somewhat unusual distinction, a more extensive definition will be useful before proceeding. In the category system used in this study, the difference between procedural and declarative knowledge in substantive episodes is based on three factors. First, for knowledge to be interpreted as procedural in the classroom setting, there must be some knowledge in the process of being constructed or developed. It is not a fait d'accompli, as in a lecture or student reading. Second, the processing is conducted by students with advice or coaching from the teacher. Without active help from a teacher, the primary function of the episode is no longer instructional. Third, the episode includes systematic use of strategies intended to enable students to transform the substantive. In the case of Mr. Gow's class (see Chapter 1), all three of these are present. In that class, students are in the process of interpreting various engravings. The teacher is providing guidance and coaching at each stage. A variety of strategies is used systematically, including rendering pictorial detail into verbal detail, comparing and contrasting to make explicit what the pictorial contrasts imply, and so forth. Not many teachers in this sample engage students in such processing.

One teacher who does is Professor Green. Because his teaching is so different from that of the other teachers in this study, the remainder of this chapter will provide an extended view and analysis of his case. Professor Green teaches at an REM campus and is one of the teachers most optimistic about the work his students are capable of. (See Chapter 3 for discussion of teacher attitude.) During our observations, Green concentrated on content not only more than anything else, but more than any other college teacher. He had divided the semester into four major sections, in each of which he focused on one type of writing. In the first, he taught what he called objective writing, what others might call expository descriptive writing with a focus on detail. In the second part he focused on "story workshop," a method developed by Schultz (1982). The third part was to be argument, but he decided against that because of lack of time. The fourth

> continues throughout the whole course and that's this book right here. It's a program, . . . a programmed text with answers at the back and they keep going through this over and over. It drills the living hell out of them. You think it would drill the living errors out of them, but it doesn't.

A programmed text is one that breaks down what is to be learned into small steps. As a student moves through the text, he or she fills in certain answers, and if the answer is correct, moves to the next frame. If the answer is wrong, the student returns to the beginning of the section to work through it again. Professor Green does not use this text in class. He simply explains how to use it and grades the students on the number of pages they have done. As it turns out, the major portion of class time is devoted to the second part, the story workshop. He explains:

> This approach requires wholly different kinds of skills than you find ordinarily in the classroom. Much more imagination. Much more sense of vision, seeing, words I use all the time in class are *seeing*, *image*, *voice*. They, lots of them don't quite catch onto that. And that's okay. That's why you do it. If they already knew it, you wouldn't be doing it.

As Professor Green explains it, the approach involves four major activities: reading pieces of writing aloud, responding to those pieces by recalling images from them and telling the images directly (he avoids "explaining" them); having students find their own images and develop them in class while Professor Green coaches; writing on the basis of some of those images, but without specific assignments, only numbers of pages; and conferring with students about the papers they have written. Like Professor Thomas, Professor Green wants students to think of their work as being "in progress." He says to his students,

> No piece that you do [is necessarily complete]. . . . Some pieces are finished and some pieces you give me, after you give them to me, even before I make comments and return them to you, you may start to think, boy, I could have said this, I could have done that, I could have done this. It's not necessarily done. You can redo a piece of it. . . . I suspect that that particular piece that you give me, though I haven't read the first two sentences, I suspect that that piece is going to be inside you, wandering around, jumping up and down and kicking and tossing for some days, and that you're going to come up with another piece that will probably be, you know, a lot longer than that piece. And richer and fuller. . . . If that piece still keeps moving inside of you and wants more done to it, do it.

As far as assignments go, Professor Green says that he gives his students a lot of freedom, but he requires 80 typewritten pages in a semester. That, he says, comes to only five pages per week. In 16 weeks he gives a dozen specified assignments. The remaining are unspecified: "Give me what you think is the most powerful thing you have not written about." When the interviewer evinced some surprise at the amount of writing required, Professor Green said, "Today I got one 26-page piece from a student and I got a 22-page piece from a student. Now that's English 100, remedial. There's nobody in this building getting 22 and 26 pages a day." To keep this amount of writing coming, he believes, he has to let students know that he values what they write:

I quietly will say to someone, like today I said to Lynette, you know, your writing has gotten so much better. She just has to hear that once in a while, not particularly her, but some others. Just let them know. . . . I said to a new student today, "You have a lot of promise," I said, "and you are not giving me stuff. Monday, I want to see your stuff." But I let him know he had promise and I could see he lit up a little bit. . . . He lit up and I thought, it's just [that] they need—those little prompts on the side.

In one class, Professor Green begins with a reading from Elia Kazan's *A Walker in the City,* a rich passage about the neighborhood in which the writer lived as a youth. Following this reading, he asks students to recall images from the story and to see them. He calls on individuals to give the image in their minds. He does not want commentary or explication, but rather, a secondary seeing. Even the casual reader will notice marked differences between these days and the portions of days we have seen in other classes so far. I will argue that the difference is more fundamental than a difference in style, technique, or teaching strategy. It is a difference in the perception of how learning takes place. To argue this difference, I believe, it is important to present the following classroom session in considerable detail. It is important, also, to note how student talk and writing become part of the basis for the intended learning. Professor Green opens the class with some business, but within a few minutes, he begins to read a piece of student writing:

PROFESSOR GREEN: (reading student's piece) I'm at home, all alone. So I look out my window, a man very young, wearing a black shirt with ACDC written on the front. I'm only 12 years old. The man is standing on a window ledge, wearing torn blue jeans. He looks very nervous. His eyes are wide open and completely red. Maybe he lacks sleep. His hair is dusty blonde and looks very dirty. His facial hair is stubby. It gives him a bumish appearance. A crowd is gathering around the house where the man is. The men and women of the crowd are staring at this man with the look of amazement. Their mouths are wide open, eyes are alert and all are fixed on the man. Policemen start to clear the crowd and speak to the man on the window ledge with a weird speaker that is attached to the officer's mouth. The police plead with the man, not to do it. I don't know what this man did, but it must be dangerous and [scary]. I continue watching. The man screams to the speculated audience. He says, "Move away, God damn ya!" He digs in his pocket and pulls out a switchblade. He holds the switchblade in his right hand and shuts his eyes as if to blank out the entire world. Why is this man doing this? Is he in trouble?

The man's hand is shaking like my grandmother's. Her hand
shakes once in a while, my father said it's because she has arthritis.
The man lets out a scream, saliva starts to come down the corners of
his lips. He looks sad and depressed. His nose is running and he
sheds tears. He takes his left hand and pulls out a clear plastic bag
with white powder inside. He throws it like a baseball into the air.
Why did he throw away sugar? He places the knife between his
palms and clings tightly. Rapidly, he inserts the knife into his
stomach and groans loudly. When he pulls the blade out, blood
covers it. He kneels down, eyes squinting, mouth grinning; he slowly
falls from the ledge of the window. The crowd looks different. Their
eyes look like they're going to pop out of their sockets. The crowd
screams and starts to run towards the man who lays next to the white
Chevette. He has blood on his face. Is he dead? I close the curtains
and run to my room. My mother will be home any minute. She
demands that my bedroom be cleaned at all times.

PROFESSOR GREEN: (stops reading and looks up) Isn't that a great last line?
Terrible incident and the mother demands that the bedroom be clean
at that time. Whose voice? Laura, whose voice? I know it's hard to
tell at this point.

(Professor Green allows students to make some guesses and then asks
them to do "recalls.")

PROFESSOR GREEN: What do you recall in that narrative? What can you see
again? Emphasis on seeing again, not on remembering. Yes?

ROBERTO: As soon you said he was wearing ACDC, I thought of . . .

PROFESSOR GREEN: What do you see in the piece though?

ROBERTO: In the piece I see—

PROFESSOR GREEN: Rather than fantasy also.

ROBERTO: When he threw the sugar up and seen it go in the air and land
on the ground. I seen that. I seen him—I didn't see blood though. I
didn't see him (inaudible). I didn't see any blood.

PROFESSOR GREEN: Okay, interesting notion here, he threw up some sugar
in the air. What did he throw in the air?

ROBERTO: Cocaine.

PROFESSOR GREEN: Probably cocaine. Probably, we don't know that
though. The reason we don't know is because the boy's point of view
is that. He doesn't leave that point of view does he? He doesn't tell
you, suddenly switch . . . to cocaine (laughter). Kids see the white
packet. That's what he tells you. It's much better that *you* complete
the meaning by knowing what it is, than that he tell you. He sees a
white bag over there. That's what he tells you. He doesn't see cocaine
in the air. We are so used to abstracting and explaining that we often

don't have to see what was there first. Okay, what else did you see? What do you recall?

RACHEL: It says when he's explaining, in the beginning, right at the beginning how that boy looks like—it's so useful because you see a lot of them, like in school. Like you see the guys with the rock shirts and they're all drugged out all the time. So that's the first picture that comes to my mind.

PROFESSOR GREEN: Uh huh, yes. See again, not what *comes* to your mind. . . . Some of you are giving the fantasies and what came to *your* mind, what you *thought* of when you heard it. This is not what I'm asking for. I'm asking for you to literally see something he gave, nothing else, not fantasy, not thought, see something in the piece. . . . All right, what do you see?

ROGER: The expression that he was slowly falling off the ledge.

PROFESSOR GREEN: Well, he pointed at it. What is the expression? What did you see?

ROGER: It brought back memories.

PROFESSOR GREEN: OK, all right. (Carlos raises his hand.) Carlos what did you see?

CARLOS: I seen when he took the knife, probably with one hand. He probably had a bloody (inaudible) on something. That was probably it, and blood was squirting out of the side, and he pulled it out. The blood was leaked from the knife. In fact, thick, like paint [like] ketchup and stainless steel, because it shines. So this reflects all from, off the stainless steel bladed knife. Then it drips in the street. The tip is all splattered with blood. He holds his hand, he holds his wound with his hand and he drops the knife. He at last falls slowly.

PROFESSOR GREEN: OK, that's a good scene. That's a good scene. All right, there's a lot more.

Obviously, what Carlos "gives" is not only what is in the original. We needn't divide these passages according to precise linguistic rules to see that Carlos has taken the original and expanded it considerably. He has added more precise details, about the blood, the knife, the man, and his actions. This is not simply a recall in the usual sense of that word. It is a reconstruction. Carlos tells us how *he* sees it. He has added details that he sees in his mind's eye, but that are not in the original. And that is precisely the kind of "scene" that Professor Green wants. Professor Green resumes:

PROFESSOR GREEN: Let's go on [to another student piece]. I want you to see this as I read it; see it; hear the voice. This one I bet you know who this is. (Reads) I turn around and try to open my eyes. There is my mother beside my bed stretching her arms to me, touching my face softly to wake me up. With a warm smile she says, "The trip honey, wake up." "It's Mother, the trip," I say and I jump off the bed to get ready. The lights are all on all over the house, and it looks like daytime. I see my mother's face and she is smiling. So I smile back at her. She appears to be happy and excited and she makes a clear statement looking at me and my brother who just has joined us.

"I want the two of you to get ready as soon as possible."

"Yes, Mother," we answered at the same time. My brother is 7 and I'm only 5. He still seems half asleep, so we head to the bathroom. In there, instead of getting ready, we start discussing who is going to be at the window seat in the train. Finally I'm ready, and our grandmother is in the kitchen waiting for us to eat breakfast. Our parents seem relaxed and nice in their sports clothes. They drink coffee and talk about the good time we are going to have in St. Augustine National Park. I looked at my grandmother, who is also drinking a cup of coffee, there's something special about her today that I cannot understand. Her fragile figure, her white hair, her slim and peaceful face, full of miracles—wrinkles. (Stops to comment: Miracles is better.) full of wrinkles and her smooth freckled hands all of a sudden look more real, more visible to me. Her eyes are fixed on mine and we look into each other's for a long while, with complete silence. My father went out to get a taxi to take us to the train station. My brother and I followed him to wait at the front door. My mother is taking the luggage to the door and only my grandmother sits alone at the table.

A few minutes after we hear my mother almost screaming, but we don't understand anything she is saying. We run inside and there is my mother kneeling on the floor, holding my grandmother's head. She looks like she's sleeping. But she is extremely pale, her mouth half open and her beautiful eyes that 10 minutes before look like clear crystal, now look like small, brown balls, wrapped in white human tissue. I start to cry and I run out looking for my father. I still can't talk. I just cry. He takes me inside and sets me on the floor where he sees what is going on. Very fast he picks her up in his arms, and in the taxi that is waiting at the door, they disappear to the hospital. Later on we meet him in a waiting room. The room is big, white and feels cold, and it smells like medicine all over. We sit and wait. After several hours a very young doctor comes out of the double doors, smiling at my parents. He says, "Thank God, everything is going to be OK." We decide to leave the hospital and go out for dinner. In the restaurant our parents promise the trip for next month. (Stops reading) OK, whose piece? Whose piece?

Professor Green again allows students to guess and then waits to hear images that students see in their mind's eye:

MARCIA: The image in my mind was the piece where the grandma was like—she looks small, but lays there with her eyes half open, her mouth half open and her eyes, all you see is like eyes are real pale white. She looks normal when you first look at her, but she's real pale looking. It's scary looking over, it makes you want to cry. You look once again and you know her mouth is half open, you wonder why she's not saying nothing and her eyes are real pale and white. It's scary looking.

PROFESSOR GREEN: OK, when you do a recall or an image, kind of skip all that preparatory material like "the thing I can remember." The thing I won't see is all that. Just give it. Just that. Okay.

ALISHA: The lady telling the kids, hurry up, let's go for the trip. I could see that. That's like, she's—that's like when you're in a rush and everything, you want to get things right away done and I could see that like hurriedness. What's that called? There's a word for that. Well anyways, whatever that word is, I could see that. The kids are like OK, OK, like rushing them.

EARNEST: You can see the table, she's staring at her grandmother and the grandmother's sitting there with, as you called them, miracles in her face.

PROFESSOR GREEN: By the way, that little accident, there is the kind of accident you ought to—when those things occur, and they do occur, be aware of the small little miracle that has happened in speech or language there. When I read *miracles* for *wrinkles*, if I had been the writer, and made that error, I'd've said, wow, let's keep that. Because it's a miracle in her face. All faces have miracles to some extent.

Professor Green builds again on the student comment as well as on his own miscue in reading. But he takes advantage of the student's noting it to provide this little lecture, so that his advice builds again on classroom events that are, in part, the students' doing. Andrea speaks next, and Professor Green will build on her comment:

ANDREA: I feel this like, maybe one time my grandma was sitting there. Nothing was said, but there was so much that was said.

PROFESSOR GREEN: Yes, yes, that's it. That's the moment really where the whole piece is. The whole piece was worth that one paragraph. That's the paragraph around which the whole piece works. It says, if that's the centerpiece and everything else doesn't matter, except one paragraph. This is that paragraph again. Everything else, as it were, leads up to it and then trails away from it. And it's that one paragraph, that's where the magic is. It's that makes the piece worth reading. (He reads.) I looked at my grandmother who is also drinking a cup of coffee. There is something special about her today, but I cannot understand. Her fragile figure, her white hair, her slim and peaceful face, full of wrinkles and her smooth freckled hands, all of a sudden look more real, more visible to me. Her eyes are fixed on mine and we look into each other's for a long while in complete silence. (He finishes reading.) Silence, when you really sit and see through silence, there's far more happening than when you listen to speech. But let me do one more thing again. Let me read one sentence in there again and look at this sentence, it's the kind of sentence you're looking for when you read. A sentence that's got flow and magic in it, instead of a blah, blah, blah, blah, blah, blah, blah. This one . . . flows like a river. Listen to it: Her fragile figure, her white hair, her slim and peaceful face, full of wrinkles and her smooth freckled hands, all of a sudden look more real, more visible to me. Hear that? Hear the rhythm in that, paralleling? Listen. Let your voice be open to those things in your sentences. . . . We've heard them. They're there. They are possible. Let your voice be open to them.

Professor Green reads another piece about a boy's first kiss. It is as strong as the first two pieces. He asks students to respond in the same way.

Before discussing the remainder of the class, I would like to comment on three features of it. First, Professor Green's positive attitude toward his students is apparent in much of what he says and needs no further comment. Second, a large proportion of his talk, aside from his reading of the student pieces, is in response to what the students have said. His decisions to develop what they say makes the students' thinking a crucial part of the knowledge-building process. He intends that his emphasis of the sentence containing parallelism, his encouragement of the imaging, his praise of various responses will help to insure that students will continue contributing to that process. Third, and perhaps most important, what the students say and write have become major learning materials in the class. Students have become part of the teaching process. In a very real sense, teacher and students are constructing knowledge together.

At this point, Professor Green has a little more than 10 minutes left in the class. He states the general themes of the three student pieces and calls them universals: drug dealing and death, an older person loved very much, and first love. He asks students to find an image in "any one of the universals, your own image." When the students appear uneasy, he decides to make it "first love":

PROFESSOR GREEN: First love, first sex, first kiss, however you want to do that, first sight of a naked body of the opposite sex, whatever, some image off of that. Universal, we'll use first love. (Hector raises his hand.) Okay, Hector, see it as you give it.

HECTOR: (He speaks extemporaneously.) When I was younger we used to play kick the can. I was usually *it* or the guy who had to chase them because I was always the youngest guy. So they just forced me to do it. . . .

PROFESSOR GREEN: I want you to go into the present tense now, so that you see it now. The game didn't happen when you were 12, your game is happening right now as you tell it.

HECTOR: Okay, they just tossed the can, everybody's hiding it now. I'm looking around for them and I know they're always hiding, like they always hide. I went in there to chase after them and I stopped and there was a blind about halfway open.

PROFESSOR GREEN: Where are you at now? You're what?

HECTOR: OK, it's going to come—OK there's like a little [space] between buildings and then right there, sort of like a backyard and there's an opening to the next block. They'd be hiding there, because it's dark. There was like a tree and then the first floor. It's right there eye level. I'm running there, and I'm running between the two to chase them to see if I could see them, so I could call John because Johnny always hides in there. And I stopped and it was blinds halfway opened, and I looked inside the blinds, and I see a lady, just laying there. She's got her underwear on. And me being a pervert, just keeps staring in there. I see a man come out in his underwear and I'm wondering whoa, wait a minute. I was curious to know what's going on here. I'm looking in there and I see the man starts kissing the lady. He starts like fondling her breasts and I'm wondering if they're going to come off or not. I'm looking out here, hey. Right, he's going to her back and then comes the bra. Sure enough, off comes the bra. Then he's just kissing her all over. She's speaking inside and she's moving her head, moaning and I hear all the guys in the next block. I hear them whispering, "Where's Hector? Where's Hector? Let's get the can. Let's get the can." I hear the can drop *tschew*, but I don't run after it.

I'm just standing there looking at them. Then the man starts holding her waist and he grabs the end of her underwear and he slips them down (laughter) and he's staring right into there like. It's—if you got the lights on, the blinds are like halfway open, and he looks like he looked up and down to get a good view of the woman. So I'm staring in there, and he's looking down, I'm looking up. In the meantime the guy his hands are moving around and the lady is letting him, and I'm wondering now what? I try [to do that], they never let me finish. (laughter) And the guy's hands moving up and down and moving around, and she's sort of just holding back like this. (Hector provides body language to demonstrate.) Maybe that's (inaudible) for her underwear, to pull them off, and like she has one ring around her leg, and he just takes the underwear, flips it off of her. Then they both jump under the covers and that's when I see like, him I guess they were using [a rubber], and two hands were shaking. He's all excited, and she was (inaudible). Then I see her, by herself another (inaudible).

PROFESSOR GREEN: Go back now, go back. See again, the blinds are—are they halfway up?

HECTOR: Well they're like—it's a 45-degree angle.

PROFESSOR GREEN: But they're all the way down, but they're turned so that you can look—

HECTOR: Well actually it's like you get the blinds up and then you move them up little, . . . you would be able to see it with this woman and it caught my eye, just stopped and looked. And I see her just waiting there for the guy to come, and she's just like waiting on the bed. She's like just waiting there, just sitting around and I see the man coming in and she's in her underwear, so I just stopped and I just stopped. I looking there and I see them. It's like the blinds are up, look down and look up, you could see it and then the light reflecting off. It's dark outside (inaudible) hands against the window, then you can see a better view of it.

PROFESSOR GREEN: It's nighttime?

HECTOR: It's nighttime.

PROFESSOR GREEN: OK, that would help me a lot. All right it's lit. It's lit and the outside is dark. So you have to put your hands against the windows if you get a better view. So you do [or] don't see your own, like reflection? (Hector nods.) Go back and look at the woman again. See her more clearly this time. What do you notice? You, out in the outside, hands to the window, through the blinds, what do you notice about that woman. First time (inaudible), at the first moment you see her, what do you focus on? What do you see?

HECTOR: I'm the (inaudible) her underwear. She's got a little bra and lacelike panties. That's the first thing that catches my eye. The first things I'm staring at. Then I look up at her face and she's got real nice makeup. She had nice long blond hair, and she looked like she just bathed or put on makeup just then. She looked so clean, so fresh. It looks like she's got her underwear on. And she got a very firm body, nice firm body.

PROFESSOR GREEN: What do you notice about the man? Look at him, his hair, his face, something, what?

HECTOR: He's got a mustache, (inaudible) like he's clean and shaved himself. He just look like he just . . . , because he's got a couple nicks, like he just shaved. And it's like he also just bathed too. He's wearing those jungle underwear (laughter). It's like jungle. It's got like a tiger, tiger shape. (Inaudible) the crotch is and then he's got like strings and then . . .

STUDENT: A G-string.

HECTOR: Not a G-string, but just little strings inside, and it's got just a (inaudible) on the buns. (Hector impersonates the man.) "No, you're not going to see me tonight. You can admire because I want to see how would you look like."

PROFESSOR GREEN: How old, how old would you think?

HECTOR: They were early, late 20s. She's still young and very attractive, and he's young, well cleaned and shaven. He's got black pushed-back hair, looks like he just got it cut or something and he's got a nice trimmed mustache, kind of thick, but trimmed. And he just shaved, (inaudible) couple nicks, and he's real clean. Then he's got his jungle underwear.

PROFESSOR GREEN: OK, that's very good, very well done. Should be that long even when all of a sudden you're watching this and in a distance you hear whispering, "Where's Hector? Where's Hector?" and the can falls. Suddenly, because that's there, we can see this better. Because there is something else, there's this into our presence. Because the jungle underwear is there, the guy is more real. It's those little things, because his face is nicked, he's freshly shaved. There's more presence because of those little things. OK, that's a good, just wonderful, and that can go on, that's not the end of that piece. You know that.

HECTOR: I hate to find out.

PROFESSOR GREEN: OK, it's unfortunate [there's no] time to do more. . . . For Monday, do a piece that comes up with the universal (inaudible) . . . first experience with sex and again it doesn't have to be first either, it's the sense of first. Whether it is first or not. It's not important. But some piece off of that for Monday. OK?

I have quoted unusually long portions of this class because it is such an unusual class and because it provides a powerful example for analysis. Before I turn to that analysis, let us hear what Professor Green himself has to say about it. We were fortunate to be able to conduct a lengthy interview with Professor Green immediately after this class. (Many times our interviews were cut short because of the busy schedules of the teachers.) In this follow-up interview, Professor Green talks about the course as a whole, Hector's work, and his own role in the class. Commenting on Hector's response, he says that Hector

> did a good job. He—one of the nice things about him is he was . . . pretty much uninhibited in giving that. He really gave it, . . . but his gestures and his body was moving in such a way that we all saw it. What he needed to was to translate that into language. . . . But where does the bobbing up and down in your head come in to the language you're giving? Because the gesture in the body is often, often saying what the words aren't. If you can find that and put that in there, then it's wonderful.

Professor Green sees his job as more than coaching students to move from the implicit to the expressed. At the heart of his coaching is his attempt to help his students achieve a certain kind of experience. In scenes such as the preceding, he is attempting, at one level, to "coach seeing and coach voice" in the teller, so that "when it comes to the writing, it's already there." However, he explains that the coaching is not only for the tellers,

> but for everyone else listening to it too. The coaching there is for them to see the scene that's there . . . and for them to hear the voice that becomes, first, a model for them and, secondly, a possibility, another possible voice that might be partly theirs, a voice that might be sad or angry. That's more permission, it's more possibility and it's modeled as well. . . . It's permission, possibility, and model. It's the experience of it. I guess that's the word I'm really trying to get at here. It's not an intellectual concept I'm discussing, it's an experience I'm trying to get them to have.

The experience that Professor Green moves his students toward is similar in some ways to the experience that Mr. Gow hopes his students will have (see Chapter 1). Both teachers hope their students will have a series of successful experiences that will enable them to use the strategies on their own, that they will hear and learn from the ideas of others and become more attuned to the impact of their own ideas, and that they will become personally committed to thoughtful work with language.

Of course, there are many differences as well. The two teachers are working quite different kinds of writing. Because Professor Green's class is working on personal narrative, the experience is one that integrates "feeling, seeing, voice, and movement." For that reason, he was pleased to note Hector's body movements, which are an indication of this integration. Professor Green also drives toward an experience that creates personal connections for writers and audiences. He points to an example from the class on that day:

> A student came up at the end. There was the piece about the grandmother who almost died. A student came up, a Black student over there. (Points to where the student had been seated.) He said, "That paragraph was wonderful, magnificent." He meant it. He was being genuine with me. He said, "She was so beautiful that woman, that grandmother." Wow! We connected for him. He had that experience because the experience was there and given, he had the experience.

Professor Green believes that students must learn to "receive the experience" in order to give it. For that reason, his coaching after readings and tellings is aimed at helping students to recall, to tell others what they have seen, as Carlos tells the class what he has seen in the suicide scene described earlier. He coaches students "to notice that experience and to have that experience as a receiver of the experience, rather than a giver of the experience." But receiving is a prelude to giving. His skilled coaching of Hector results in not only a solid first-round telling, but also a revision of it that supplies the little details that make it real, that make it present. Professor Green believes that "if they once have the experience [of giving], then they're capable of having it any other time, when they write."

It is important to note that this is not simply a mystical experience. Professor Green is careful to see that his coaching includes the use of models that incorporate the kinds of detail that he is after. He praises Carlos's reconstruction of the suicide scene, one that adds to the details in another student's writing. He praises the details included in both pieces read aloud, details that help to maintain the point of view. In Hector's telling, he guides Hector to find more detail that make the man and woman come alive. Clearly, from a strategic point of view, every class is focused on generating highly specific language that conveys feeling and emotion. In addition, he takes time to read and reread a sentence filled with parallelisms that demonstrate a method of incorporating those details into the writing.

THE HEART OF THE DIFFERENCE

The case of Professor Green contrasts in many ways with the other examples and cases examined up to this point. First, with this remedial class, he chooses to focus on relatively few kinds of writing, three, to be precise, and a programmed text for teaching punctuation and usage, and he decides to drop argument in order to have more time for story workshop.

Second, he simply refuses to spend class time on mechanics. He says,

> I have found that English 100 classes here have a lot of potential . . . , [but] teachers get so involved with teaching grammar, punctuation, spelling, mechanics, that real life is never touched.

He says that he marks all the mechanical problems they have, but more important, he says, he also writes something about what the student "really said." He explains,

> I want them to know that, you know, "You've got something going for you. Why do you screw it up with these little errors? You can clean that up. You know you can." They begin to, when they know they can, and they see what the problems are. Repeatedly, they clean it up.

Third, his classroom focus is almost exclusively on substance (professional models, student writing, and student tellings and recalls). Further, that concentration on substance is nearly exclusively devoted to the procedural. Even though we would code a reading aloud as declarative, the purpose of the reading is for learning procedures.

These differences are clearly connected to his optimism about his students' potential, an optimism that is reflected in line after line of his interviews with us. But perhaps as important in accounting for the differences is his stance toward learning. He does not make this stance explicit, but it is implicit in much of what he says about student learning. Simply put, he believes that learning is a constructive act. He does not use that term; but if we listen carefully to his talk, we find that the constructive assumption is present. The essential evidence of that is his talk about the experience that he hopes his students will have. The experience is not simply recall, but a reseeing, a construction of the image that the student recalls.

Professor Green's main effort is to engage students in the experience of receiving and giving stories. The reception of the stories, as the example given here illustrates, entails reconstructing them from one's own point of view. Giving a story is clearly an act of construction. Further, Professor Green sees his work as that of setting the conditions that will enable students to have the experience necessary to receiving and giving. He knows that he cannot tell them how to do it. He knows that he can select the materials that may prompt such experiences but that he must cajole and coach students into the experience. But the experience itself, he believes, must be theirs.

We see this attitude in some of the optimistic teachers from time to time. For example, Professor Thomas nudges her students toward construction of revisions. We see it in the classroom of teachers who use problem-solving group work, in which students are to develop their own solutions. But for the most part it is missing from those who are not optimistic.

For most teachers in the sample, teaching is an act of telling, as though they are able to transfuse their ideas directly into the minds of students. And when the ideas do not hold, it is simply that students have not applied themselves to the task of learning what was put forward for them to learn. These teachers appear to believe that teaching is objective, that what is to be learned may be laid out, and that learners can listen and learn, as though the knowledge is directly absorbable into the mind, without transformation. Many teachers in the sample adopt this objectivist stance.

On the other hand, teachers such as Professor Green and Mr. Gow believe that teachers cannot simply tell students what is to be learned and expect them to learn it. They suggest that students must themselves be active agents in their own learning, transforming what is to be learned through the screen of their own experience and existing understandings. They believe that to be successful, learners must construct or reconstruct, for themselves, what is to be learned. They adopt a constructivist stance toward teaching and learning.

This distinction between objectivist and constructivist stances is at the heart of differences between these teachers. It is not the task in this study to discover how or even why teachers develop one stance or the other. That is a matter for future research. The difference, however, appears to be one of the most important that we encounter.

❦ 6 ❦

The Construction of Curriculum

TWO IMPORTANT PARTS OF Shulman's (1986, 1987) and Grossman's (1990) concept of pedagogical content knowledge have to do with knowledge of curriculum and knowledge of strategies and representations available "for teaching particular subject matter" (Grossman, 1990, p. 9). Both Shulman and Grossman appear to suggest that teachers recall this information for use in the classroom. The examples presented so far, however, suggest that the situation is more complex than that. Throughout the previous chapters, I have hypothesized that teachers develop or adapt curricular structures on the basis of their own views of the students whom they teach and their ideas about the nature of learning. Even when teachers use a textbook with some care, as Professor James appears to do, or follow curriculum guidelines closely, what happens in class is likely to be based on the teachers' own interpretations of the text or curricular guidelines. The curricular structures that we have seen so far support that hypothesis.

Let us examine that hypothesis carefully to consider more precisely what it involves. The expression *subject matter for teaching* is a combination of several different notions. The widest sense of the subject matter may be thought of as whatever falls within the interests of those teaching that subject, the canonical and noncanonical alike, and perhaps what they have not thought to be interested in yet. In schools, there is a tendency to narrow this very broad conception to the content of the textbooks and curriculum guides or even to some more specific selection of these. Anyone teaching a subject must, of necessity, make some selection of the wider subject matter available for teaching, which may or may not be congruent with the subject as it appears in textbooks and guides. In Chapters 3 and 4 I argued that teachers' perceptions of their students as learners affect the concrete or instrumental goals adopted and that these, in turn, control what is taught and how it is evaluated. I argue in Chapter 5 that the stance taken toward teaching and learning appears to have a powerful impact on the microcurriculum, the kinds of activities included. In addition, however, we will see that the selection of subject matter and its reconstruction for teaching is heavily based on the teachers' views of the sequence in which learning takes place.

To examine this expanded hypothesis, we will look at two cases, to examine more closely the factors influencing the construction of curriculum. The cases presented in earlier chapters include instances of teachers' concentrating on formal discourse knowledge (characteristics and features of kinds of writing) and others of teachers' concentrating on substantive knowledge in both declarative and procedural modes. The two cases that follow provide instances of teachers who focus on discourse at the level of mechanics and usage but do so in quite different ways.

PROFESSOR DOBBS

Professor Dobbs, a teacher at a PW campus, considers his students in English 100 to be unprepared as readers and writers and unable to deal with more than a few specified and limited tasks at a time. In contrast to Professor Green, he deems the essential goal of the course to be learning the conventions of "standard edited prose" so that they can be used automatically. All of the instruction, evaluation, and practice move toward that end. During the first year of observations, 98% of the observed instructional time was devoted to such work on mechanics and syntax.

The Subject Matter Focus

Professor Dobbs explains that because his students make so many mistakes in mechanics and usage, he does not "teach a type of writing." He explains that the students he works with have been placed in English 100 on the basis of a "placement test because they cannot write standard edited English." Because he is trying to establish habits of writing standard edited English, he works only with narrative writing. His curricular goal for English 100 is to teach so that his students "overlearn" the conventions of punctuation and standard edited English to the point that they become habit. He sees this automaticity as highly important for students to develop before they go on to writing.

Learning Theory

At some point in his career, Professor Dobbs "became very much interested . . . in how you develop the kind of expertise that world-class athletes have." He believes that "the training techniques, both physical and mental, for becoming a world-class athlete, seem . . . to have very obvious applications to the kinds of things we [are] trying to teach here [in English 100]." In his thinking about this problem, he was influenced by an article on the coaching techniques of John Wooden in *Psychology Today*. He says,

> I realized the description that was given of him was the kind of thing I thought made up good teaching. And so I began more and more to work in

that direction, and now I'm firmly committed. I'm sure that is without doubt *the way* to teach English. . . . What I am after is to get the student to do something right and then to practice it over and over and over again. . . . Once you've learned to do something right, you haven't learned much yet, and the mistake that most textbooks make is that as soon as the student is able to do something right, they go on to some more complicated problem and try to mess him up as quickly as possible, with the result that he never really learns much of anything.

He goes on to argue the benefits of overlearning, using evidence drawn from the process of learning music; a study of attempts to use standard English instead of the speaker's normal dialect; and personal experience in trying to write with the left hand. The basic idea, one advanced by various writers (e.g., Hirsch, 1982), is that of cognitive overload; that is, when one is engaged in new tasks demanding new skills, established skills deteriorate. According to Professor Dobbs, these deteriorate because

there is very definitely a limit to what we can monitor at any one time. So your attention is focused on sentence structure, punctuation, verb forms, and so on, you're going to leave out all the other things, which I think are much more important in the long run.

To develop habits of correctness, he uses the same "techniques" that are used in athletics,

where you don't have a swimming team sitting around the pool and discuss swimming techniques. You don't have them read a book on swimming. You put them in the pool and they swim back and forth over and over.

You have to begin, he says, with helping the student "to do something right" in the first place.

Curricular Structures

The outline of Professor Dobbs's course is not very different from the outline of the grammar course that was frequently taught 40 years ago at the freshman level in many universities: the sentence and its punctuation, phrases and their punctuation, punctuating quotations, and so forth. This selection of topics may be thought of as the macro level of the curriculum. At this level, we may think of Professor Dobbs as selecting from preexisting curricula so that little construction is involved. However, at the micro level, at the level of how these topics are treated, Professor

Dobbs's lessons are clearly his own construction. Working within the traditional range of topics for courses focused on mechanics and usage, and within his analogy of the development of world-class athletes through practice, he admits that the next question concerns how one helps students "to do something right" in the first place. He explains that "at the very lowest level, which is our 98 class, what I did was have them do a lot of copying, just plain copying." He points out that "this was really very difficult for them because they would make all kinds of mistakes in the copying." He believes that copying helped students learn

> to put capital letters at the beginnings of sentences, to put periods in certain places. You had indentations in paragraphs and all that sort of thing.

I asked, "But when they couldn't copy correctly, what did you do?" Without hesitation, he replied,

> Then you had them do it over again until they got it correct. In other words, . . . they had to realize that the variations they made between what was there and what they had put on the paper were important. They couldn't just go ahead and make those variations at will.

At the higher level of English 100, he uses what he regards as the more demanding "techniques" of "dictation and imitation":

> We give them passages which actually are from Hemingway's *A Farewell to Arms* which I have rewritten and edited, and we dictate the passages in the class. They have them to study, and a week later we will dictate them. And the dictation is for a couple of purposes. One is again the practice of writing things correctly, but the other is that I think there is really a lot of value in training them to relate what they write to the way they normally talk.

Because he believes that "these students have no real experience with writing and with relating what they read to what they say," the "flow of speech that goes through their minds" can provide very few cues about what should appear on paper:

> They have to learn, for example, in the phrase *in the bed of the river*, what does *bed of* the mean? They have to learn to spell *bed of the*. They have to learn to make a distinction between /ən/ meaning *in* and /ən/ meaning *and*. It's the same sound in normal conversation, but it's a big difference in spelling when you write, and it has consequences for punctuation, because if it's an *and*, you might put a comma in front of

it, if it's *in*, you'd probably put a period and a capital *I* on it, depending on where it's located in the flow of speech. So the dictation has that as a major purpose, to help them relate the way they normally talk to the way they would write.

In dictating, therefore, Professor Dobbs reads "the whole passage through at normal conversational level, normal intonation and mispronunciation." He says that he is less careful about pronouncing in dictation than he is "in normal speech"

because I figure most of my students are less careful in pronunciation. Like for example the word *frost*, which I would probably pronounce with a *t* on the end, I very carefully pronounce without a *t* on the end when I'm dictating, because that would be the way most of my students would talk, and I want them to realize that the flow of conversational speech that goes through their minds when they write is all they've got to tell them what to put on the paper.

The dictation helps students see the relationship between reading and writing, and "it's a means of giving them something that they can do correctly." Moreover, he said,

each passage that we use [in dictation] appears in about three forms. The first form will be rewritten so that it has only simple sentences. Then a little later we'll give them the same passage but now written so that it has a couple of compound sentences in there. And then written again so that it has complex sentences, so that they get different punctuation problems as they progress. More and more they become familiar with the words, so the words do not become a problem, but it's the voice pattern, the rhythm, the intonation patterns, that they begin to associate with punctuation.

"So you dictate these passages more than once to them," I said, and he replied,

I will read the passage over and over and over again on a given day, 25, 30, 40 times until they've all got it. . . . We have sets of three [passages] so it will take us, say, three class meetings to get through them and then we will do them a second time. So it's about a week and a half, 2 weeks later, we'll go through the passage again. Another week and a half, 2 weeks after that, we'll go through the passage a third time, but each time in a slightly different form with respect to the punctuation and the kind of coordinate sentences or the coordinating conjunctions or subordinating conjunctions that are used.

"How much of the semester is devoted to that?" I asked. "It goes on," said Dobbs,

> up until the last 4 weeks of the semester. And the reason it stops at the last 4 weeks of the semester is that those 4 weeks are devoted to writing papers which really determine whether or not the student goes on into 101.

Professor Dobbs uses the same passages in a technique that he calls imitation. Here, he asks students to imitate the syntactic structures in each of the three versions of the passages. He provides the following example:

> Hemingway's *A Farewell to Arms* starts off something like, "The late summer of that year, we lived in a house in the village that looked across the river and the plain to the mountains. In the bed of the river there were pebbles, dry and white in the sun, and the water was clear and blue," and so on. What I want them to do is give me the same sentence pattern. The very same, in other words, "In late August of 1986 I lived in an apartment that looked across the park to the street and the supermarket," so that they're very close. The reason I want them to be close is that then they are going to be doing the punctuation correctly by imitating the model, and they will be learning to put details together in a good way.

In addition to using the techniques of copying, dictation, and imitation, Professor Dobbs lectures extensively on mechanics. In one class, when he is not dictating passages, he still has 97% of the lines. In the following class excerpt, Professor Dobbs explains,

> The conventional, not the only, but the conventional way to handle people in writing, especially when you're telling a story, is to start a new paragraph each time there's a shift to a new person. In this case we have one person talking and another person talking back to him, and so we're going to have two paragraphs. You've got to remember that's two indentations, one on the first line where you begin. Then you're going to have another one a little later. . . . Then of course there's the problem of locating the quotation marks in the right place with respect to the words, which words are actually being spoken by somebody other than the author, the words you would have heard if you'd been there, and then locating with respect to other punctuation marks, such as periods and commas. They've all got to be in the right place. OK, remember to let your margin run all the way from the top to the bottom.

He reads a passage from Stephen Crane's "The Open Boat," changing voices to denote different characters. He reads it 10 times, while students write it out and punctuate it. Then he continues his lecture:

> OK, let's go over that slowly. The expression, the injured captain, with -*ed* on the end of *injured*, it's not a past tense, it's what is called a past participle in most books. . . . It has to have an -*ed* on the end of it, even though it's not a past tense verb. . . . Now at this point, there's a voice signal. What we have next is what our book calls a half sentence, we get to that in chapter 9. Half sentences normally occur at the beginnings of sentences or the end of sentences, but they may also occur between the subject and predicate, this is what I call the wedged-in position, and when that happens most of the times there are going to be two commas around them, not one but two. And the voice signal that you're looking for is the one between *captain* and *lying*. You make a voice signal at that point that you want two commas. Don't worry about the voice signal after the word *boat*, that's going to happen anyway. Whether or not you have a comma. But the voice signal between *captain* and *lying* tells you whether or not you want zero commas or two commas, not one. Zero or two. "The injured captain, lying in the bow of the open boat," there's a change in pace, a change in rhythm, or some kind of change at that point. So we need a comma. Lying, *l-y-i-n-g*, "lying in the bow of the open boat, spoke with something strange in his voice." The voice drops, that's the end of the sentence. Now, the next word is being spoken by the captain. That is what we would have heard if we'd actually been there at the time, so now a direct quotation begins, we need quotation marks. (Reads in a different voice, the captain's) "Keep her a little more south, Billy," (in his normal voice) "he said." Now the last two words, "he said," are from the author, Stephen Crane. That's not the captain talking, so we don't have quotation marks around that.

This disquisition on the passage from "The Open Boat" continues for another 85 lines of transcript, not counting three more readings of the passage.

During the final 4 weeks of the course, students write eight narratives that include dialogue with two people talking, to demonstrate that they have learned the conventions. To move to English 101, students must earn grades of C or better on four of these.

> I'll say OK, now write about what you had for breakfast this morning or write about something that happened on the way to school or write about the last time you made a phone call or write about the last time you went

shopping, in other words very immediate experiences that they had and they just put down the details for that.

Professor Dobbs explains that "two of them actually have to be in the last 2 weeks, so many students finish the course a week early." Professor Dobbs claims that this situation

> gives me time to concentrate and give a lot of help, sort of under the table, to the students who are left the last week. . . . At that point there's no dictation going on. There's really no instruction going on except as the student comes to me for help with a paper. I tell him I won't help him, but I tell him there are various ways he can get around [that] if he'll ask me questions in the right way, and then I kind of use my judgment to decide how much to violate my prohibition against helping him, because once again, the whole purpose of this is to teach the student, not to test him. I could test him quickly, but it's to teach him, and if by putting the pressure on him, saying, "This paper is very important. You don't do well on this paper, you don't go to 101," he really focuses his attention on that. And I can maybe teach him something there that I wasn't able to teach him earlier in the semester, because he really focuses his attention.

I asked, "And . . . the criterion that you're making use of in evaluating those pieces of writing has to do with the number of errors?" His reply:

> Well, I don't count the errors. It's just that, well, I suppose in a sense I do because they have to be virtually all correct. I don't accept any errors at all to get an A. Now a few errors, and they will get down to a C. If there are a lot of errors, then they, it just isn't going to pass.

PROFESSOR KRAMER

Professor Kramer teaches English 98, a lower level of remedial English than English 100. Various teachers claim that students placed in this course have reading levels well below seventh grade. Nonetheless, Professor Kramer's expectations for her students are quite positive. She believes that their backgrounds have not prepared them for college work but that they can do the work if she can find appropriate ways to work with them. She says that her major goal for the course is "to enable the students to write, to communicate their thought effectively in a paragraph." Like Professor Dobbs, she is very much concerned with mechanics. Unlike him, however, she ties work on mechanics and syntax into her work on writing.

Learning Theory

Professor Kramer says that she avoids drill and attempts to deal with the problems she sees in the students' writing. At the same time, however, she sees a need to explicate rules thoroughly for the class as a whole. At other times she individualizes instruction. She says,

> I teach the grammar only incidentally, as they need it. I try to individualize grammatical concerns. Which is the reason at the bottom of each page I write precisely what the student needs to work on based on errors in the paper. . . . I try to meet with each student individually rather than simply return the paper. At this level the student doesn't always know what all this means. So I try to arrive in class early and stay longer and find opportunities even within the class session when the students are working in groups. I will have the student sit next to me and go over the paper with the student.

Professor Kramer also believes that it is important for her to engage students in writing that is of interest to them. In fact, she claims that

> students write best when they're enthused about their topic, and so normally I try to generate some kind of discussion and some kind of enthusiasm for the topic, you know, before they ever begin to write.

Although she is concerned with "correctness," in contrast to Professor Dobbs, she is also concerned with helping students convey their ideas effectively in writing. In English 98, this means developing paragraphs with appropriate topic sentences and support. She says,

> I do believe in focusing on writing. I don't believe in giving grammar quizzes. It tells me nothing. So that . . . , as I tell the students, the real test is whether they can write correctly . . . but [write] . . . to communicate their thought effectively. At this level, English 98, I concentrate on the paragraph. I feel that if these students can write an effective paragraph, then they can go on to English 100 and begin to extend paragraph writing to the essay.

Professor Kramer's theory of learning and teaching is based on an amalgam of the objectivist and constructivist stances discussed at the end of the previous chapter. The former permits her to lecture on rules of usage and "correctness," and the latter permits her to individualize instruction, to attempt to engage students in the topics of the writing she assigns, to engage them in peer editing and revision, and to rely on them to help generate topic ideas. This amalgam is not unusual in our sample of 19, especially for women, several of whom use both objectivist and constructivist methods. However, we see no signs of such constructivist activities in the teaching of such professors as Rose and Dobbs.

Curriculum Structures

Although Professor Kramer is very much concerned with the mechanics of writing, she does not see correctness as a prerequisite to writing, as do several teachers in our sample. Teachers who see it as a prerequisite ask students to do little or no writing, and that little is comparable to the kinds of copying and writing "about what you had for breakfast this morning or . . . about something that happened on the way to school" that we see in Professor Dobbs's curriculum. Rather, she treats writing as a concomitant to learning discourse knowledge about paragraph structure. She assumes that if students find writing meaningful and interesting, they will be more motivated to garner the mechanical skills needed to eliminate errors in mechanics and usage. Although she focuses on mechanics, she also is generally optimistic about the abilities of her students to contribute to their own learning through brainstorming topic ideas and maintaining journals to call upon for ideas to use in later writing. On occasion, she allows student ideas to become the focus of attention. This same optimism allows her to use group-editing techniques on the students' own writing, not simply on exercises to provide practice in eliminating errors of specified kinds.

Professor Kramer's curriculum focuses primarily on formal and mechanical discourse knowledge; but on occasion, in instances of brainstorming topics, she ventures into dealing with substance. Observations indicate that Professor Kramer spends time brainstorming for topics and discussing possibilities to generate interest. She devotes time to formal discourse knowledge, for example, the characteristics of "a good paragraph." She also spends considerable time on mechanics, 38.5% and 27.7% of instructional time during the 2 years of observation.

For example, Professor Kramer, in the first year of observations, fills one class with three episodes of declarative knowledge. One is a 50-minute lecture, consisting of about 600 lines of transcript, on nouns and pronouns as subjects, on verbs, prepositional phrases, and the problems of agreement. She incorporates this lecture because, she says, so many students have problems with subject-verb agreement. The following segment of the lecture groups together regular and irregular verbs:

So, what do we mean, understand then what we mean by third-person singular. That means we are speaking about one other person or thing.

And guess what, that's what we normally do. Normally when we write paragraphs and essays, we are talking about either one other person or thing, or several other persons or things. And whenever we talk about one other person or thing, we must remember to add *s* to that verb in the present tense. And adding *s* to a verb does not make it plural. Adding *s* to a noun makes it plural. Adding *s* to a verb does just the opposite. It makes it singular. So I walk to school, you walk to school, but Mary *walks* to school. And her little lamb *walks* with her because it *follows* her to school each day. And so whether our subject is a noun like *Mary*, or a *lamb*, in the present tense we've got to add *s* to the verb. Let's take another verb, let's take our verb *have*. I *have* a dog named Ginger, you *have* a cat named Puff, but Mary *has* a little lamb. Notice what's happening as soon as we get to, as soon as we speak about one other person. Whether we use the proper noun *Mary*, we've got to capitalize her name, or whether we use the common noun *girl* or *student*, or whether we use the pronoun *she*, as soon as we talk about one other person, we've got to use the verb that ends in *s*. She *has* a little lamb. And it *follows* her to school each day.

This 50-minute lecture is followed by two episodes based on work sheets, of 10 minutes and 7 minutes each, in which Professor Kramer explains how to use the information in the lecture to identify verbs, subjects, and prepositional phrases and to select the verb form that results in subject-verb agreement.

In addition, Professor Kramer spends considerable class time on both formal discourse knowledge and writing-process elements. In the class following the one just described, she lectures on the "principles" of writing a good paragraph for 19 minutes and proceeds to project students' written papers on an overhead projector for the students to evaluate under her direction. Finally, the students work in small groups on evaluating and revising papers that they have written. They are to bring to bear the principles for evaluating the formal qualities of the paragraph and the knowledge they have of subject-verb agreement. Professor Kramer lists problems at the bottom of the student papers and requires them "to take the paper to the Audio Visual Tutorial Lab, show it to the tutor, ask the tutor also to go over the paper. . . . Then the tutor will give the student . . . a supplementary . . . text . . . or a tape to listen [to,] to help instruct [them on these problems]." Thus, we may say that Professor Kramer's curriculum is both more diverse and more complex than that of Professor Dobbs. She brings formal and mechanical knowledge together, assuming that for mechanics to be meaningful, students must be engaged in meaning making. At the same time, however, her lecture on subject-verb agreement presents the same kind of fine-grained explanation that we find in Professor Dobbs's lecture on punctuating dialogue.

CURRICULUM KNOWLEDGE AND
THE DEVELOPMENT OF CURRICULUM

What I hope cannot have escaped the reader to this point are the vast differences among the major cases presented: Mr. Gow and Professors Rose, James, Green, Dobbs, and Kramer. Grossman's (1990) language in describing her category of curricular knowledge suggests a common core of knowledge that teachers hold. Her category includes "knowledge of curriculum materials available for teaching particular subject matter" and knowledge about the "horizontal and vertical curricula for a subject" (p. 8). She says that English teachers, for example, "draw upon their knowledge of which books and topics are typically addressed in the ninth grade and how the various strands of a ninth-grade curriculum might be organized" (p. 8).

If that were true, if teachers did form curriculum from knowledge of what is typically addressed in particular courses, we would expect the formulation of curricula by one teacher to have much in common with the formulations of another. In this sample of teachers, however, those formulations have very little in common, other than similarities of general topics. Thus, we see three teachers teaching essays of classification, three teaching subject-verb agreement, and two teaching narrative, but seldom are there more than 3 of the 19 teaching the same topic, and never in the same way. This knowledge of curricula, then, must be highly abstract and may be characterized as a list of optional topics that makes up the macro level of curriculum.

This list of optional topics appears to allow for considerable latitude in the final choice of what will be taught. At the macro level three of the most comparable curricula are those of Professors Danziger, James, and Rose. These professors focus on types of writing as conceptualized in current traditional rhetoric: narrative, classification, cause and effect, evaluation, and so forth. Even so, they do not all use the same types and they treat them quite differently at the micro level. That is, the kinds of information imparted, the activities used, and even the assignments are quite different. Many teachers use the topics of current traditional rhetoric combined with a list of topics from mechanics and usage. Some, like Professor Dobbs, focus on the latter and ignore the former. Still other teachers focus on neither types of writing nor mechanics but on the generation of the substance for writing within some type, as do Professor Green and Mr. Gow.

In my experience with high school and college teachers, the development of curricula by topic is very common. In one school, for example, 10th-grade teachers reached a consensus on mandatory topics and one play to be "covered" in that grade: vocabulary, the short story, poetry, the novel, *Julius Caesar*, the sentence, the paragraph, expository writing, persuasive writing, and the research paper. This list, along with a list of a recommended anthology, composition book, and set of novels, from which teachers might choose selections, made up "the curriculum" for the grade. Statements of specific goals, procedures for teaching, ways of integrating the topics, and methods of evaluation were never considered. No order for the topics was considered, and, in fact, the order varied widely partly because of book availability. In short, developing the macrocurriculum is a matter of selecting topics and books to be "covered."

Why is it that some teachers select some topics and ignore others? This is not an easily answered question. It appears that teachers develop strong commitments to certain topics in a somewhat idiosyncratic way. Although we may not be able to answer the question of why teachers develop their commitments, we can examine some of the assumptions underlying them.

In the cases above and in those presented in the preceding chapters, we can identify several assumptions that appear to guide the production of both the micro- and macro-curricula. We have already seen that teachers tend to simplify their curricular designs when they believe that their students are weak. Others, who are optimistic about their students, tend to make their curricula more complex (see Chapters 3 and 4). We have seen that some teachers focus on explanations (declarative knowledge), assuming the necessity of those explanations, whereas others focus on engaging students in tasks (procedural knowledge), assuming that without this engagement, students will not learn the necessary strategies. We have also seen that some teachers focus on strategies for developing content (Gow and Green), assuming that this process must precede learning about the formal features of written discourse and will help to take care of them.

Another important assumption has to do with what we might call fragmentation, the assumption that it is necessary to separate out parts of a whole writing task for teaching. Every teacher in the community college sample and Mr. Gow assume that some level of fragmentation is necessary. Professor Dobbs separates out various mechanical tasks for teaching, for example, punctuating dialogue. Professor Kramer concentrates on writing the paragraph. Mr. Gow separates out procedures of interpretation. Later he will attend to writing about interpretations. Professor Green focuses on narrative and leaves mechanics for work in a programmed text to be done outside class. At the same time, most teachers integrate certain features of the writing tasks. Both Green and Gow are concerned with content and how it is expressed. Professor Kramer, although focusing on the paragraph, has her students deal with both mechanics and substance in their editing session.

However, there is a qualitative difference between the kind of fragmentation engaged in by Dobbs and Kramer and that engaged in by Gow and Green. At the heart of the difference is the fact that both Gow and Green are preparing students for immediate, full-blown writing tasks. Dobbs and Kramer, on the other hand, make use of highly restricted writing tasks, which are conceived of as preparation for full-blown tasks that will arise only in the fairly distant future, namely, next semester. Such restrictions seem to me to be evidence of what has been called a building-block theory of curriculum, a theory that we commonly see in elementary and secondary school language arts programs. Generally, this theory holds that simpler elements of what is to be learned must be learned before using them in more complex structures. Thus, handwriting and spelling precede sentences, sentences precede paragraphs, paragraphs precede longer compositions, and in at least one high school curriculum "the 500-word theme" is required in the junior year, whereas "the 1,000-word theme" is relegated to the senior year. We even see such building-block curricula institutionalized as a result of state-level writing assessments. In one school system, for example, a high-school English department requires that ninth-grade students master paragraph writing in order to prepare for a tenth-grade assessment that requires multiple paragraph themes. The building-block theory has been with us for a long time and exercises a strong influence in many classrooms.

The building-block theory is not the same as movement from simple to complex tasks, though it may appear to be the same. The building-block conception of curriculum involves fragmentation of writing tasks and the assumption that students cannot move ahead until they have mastered most or all of the elements into which the task has been analyzed at a given level. However, it is possible to provide a simple learning task without dividing a task into component elements. For example, Mr. Gow engages his students first in interpreting Gilray's *Voluptuary*, a task that he sees as far simpler than the interpretation of the two engravings by Hogarth (see Chapter 1). Professor Green believes that the recalls he encourages from students after his reading of passages are easier than recalls done independently on the basis of one's own experience. In both cases, neither the easier nor the more difficult task are fragments of tasks. Both are complete tasks of a similar kind.

There is another distinction to be made between fragmented building-block curricula and focusing on specific skills. Professor Danziger includes episodes on the use of absolute phrases (see Chapter 2). He wants students to see how to use such phrases because they constitute a very important means of incorporating detail into narrative. Although in a sense the activity of working on absolute phrases constitutes a fragment of a task, Professor Danziger tells students to include such phrases in their narratives. The association of the absolute-phrase lesson with the assigned narrative integrates the lesson with actual writing. In the same way, if Professor Green were to take the time to teach punctuation of dialogue, so that students could do that in the narratives they are writing, we could not regard such a lesson as fragmented. Certainly, neither of these examples is isolated from real writing tasks in the same way as are the mechanics lessons taught by teachers who require no writing until all the mechanics have been covered.

Another factor responsible for curricular variation appears to be personal commitment to texts, ideas, or parts of a subject matter. I had a professor, for example, who was devoted to *Moby Dick*. He taught 12 texts in an American literature course and devoted the first 8 weeks of the semester to *Moby Dick* and covered the remaining 11 texts in the remaining 8 weeks. There, commitments appear to be the result of some personal experience. Professor Dobbs, for instance, explains his belief that students must overlearn skills to the point of automaticity. He also tells us that this commitment stems from his own experience in sports and his attention to what coaches do.

In Chapter 7, I will examine these and other factors and their interactions, in an effort to understand more fully how teacher thinking results in diverse curricula.

❦ 7 ❦

The Dynamics of Teacher Thinking

So FAR IN THIS BOOK I have examined several dimensions of teacher thinking: knowledge of students, conceptions of learning, pedagogical content knowledge, and knowledge of goals and curriculum. The questions remain: What are the relationships between these types of teacher knowledge? How are they organized? In addition, I have attempted to examine the problem of epistemological stance. In this chapter, I will begin by examining epistemological stance and the ways in which it relates to the categories of teacher knowledge. Then, I will turn to major relationships among all these factors.

EPISTEMOLOGICAL STANCE AND RHETORIC

In Chapter 1, I argued that a major factor determining differences in the macro- and microcurricula of various classrooms is the epistemological stance of the teacher. The majority of teachers we observed adopt an objectivist stance. This stance is characterized by lecture and the expectation that students will translate the teachers' words into actions. Thus, lectures, as we have seen across the sample as a whole and in the cases of Professors Rose, James, Thomas, Dobbs, Kramer, and Wade, constitute the main activity of the objectivist classroom. An important assumption is that the information given in lecture format can be translated into the various procedures that students must use to write not only for the course involved, but for other situations as well.

For the objectivist group as a whole, classroom exceptions are the mechanics and usage exercises, which generally follow extensive lectures, but which engage students in the procedures of finding and correcting problems in mechanics, though not content. Such exercises, of course, are objectivist in that they demand that students follow precise rules and apply them in the context of sentences constructed for that purpose. That is to say, students are not engaged in the construction of meaning but in the algorithmic application of rules.

The constructivist stance taken by Mr. Gow and Professor Green, on the other hand, results in a totally different kind of microcurriculum, one in which the students are at the center of the classroom activity. Both Mr. Gow and Professor Green believe that telling their own knowledge is inadequate for their students to attain the process oriented goals they have set. Mr. Gow believes that his students must engage in the careful observation of images, their comparison, their contrast with other images, interpreting their relationships, and so forth, in order to become expert at interpretation. Professor Green believes that his students must experience what is involved in re-creating the images of remembered experience to become skilled at writing about personal experience. He intends his coaching to develop the experience of hearing "the voice that becomes . . . permission, possibility, and model."

Both these teachers, therefore, consciously devise activities that will engage the students in experiences that entail particular strategies for developing the content of writing. Yet the strategies that these two strive to develop in their students are divergent, and their students use them for quite different purposes and in quite different constructions. The epistemological stance of the two teachers, examined in this way, does not appear to explain the differences in their larger curricular goals.

However, if we examine the teachers through the lens provided by James A. Berlin, one that ties rhetorical theories to epistemology, we will have a better understanding of the differences. Berlin (1982) outlines four major pedagogical theories in contemporary rhetoric. These are theories of the subject matter to be taught, along with their associated epistemological stances:

1. Classical rhetoric, derived from the *Rhetoric* of Aristotle
2. Current-traditional rhetoric, deriving from the Scottish commonsense realists of the 18th century
3. What I will call expressivist rhetoric, with its source, according to Berlin, in Emerson and other transcendentalists, and ultimately in Platonic philosophy
4. The "new rhetoric" or "epistemic rhetoric," with its source, according to Berlin, in rhetorics of "I. A. Richards, Kenneth Burke and the philosophical statements of Susan Langer, Ernst Cassirer, and John Dewey" (p. 773)

Berlin discriminates between these according to the approach to truth that they represent. The first two may be thought of as objectivist and the second two as constructivist.

None of the teachers in the present sample fall into the category of classical rhetoric, which Berlin considers to be "located in the rational operation of the mind" (1982, p. 773). The underlying assumption of this rhetoric is that truth can be deduced, much as one deduces theorems from axioms, corollaries, and other theorems in Euclidean geometry. According to Berlin (1982), for Aristotle, "the material world exists independently of the observer and is knowable through sense impressions." However, to "arrive at true knowledge, it is necessary for the mind to perform an operation on sense data." According to Berlin, this operation "amounts to the appropriate use of syllogistic reasoning" (p. 766). However, Aristotle wrote his *Rhetoric* to deal with arguments in which syllogistic reasoning is impossible because either the major or the minor premise is not available, as is the case in arguments that attempt to establish the facts of a case, make judgments, or determine policy (that is, determine what should be done in particular circumstances). Even here, however, arriving at conclusions is a matter of the mind's rational operation. We can expect a teacher who takes this stance to lecture, to assume that reality is directly apprehensible, and to emphasize logic, probably as syllogism, perhaps as enthymeme.

Nearly all teachers in the present sample have committed themselves to some version of current traditional rhetoric. The underlying epistemological assumption of this rhetoric is that reality may be apprehended directly through the senses. Truth is arrived at inductively, rather than deductively. Early versions of this rhetoric focused on the modes of writing (description, narration, exposition, and persuasion) but after the beginning of the 20th century, college composition began to focus on a single mode, exposition. Textbooks that focused on exposition dealt with types of exposition: definition, classification, comparison-contrast, examples, cause and effect, evaluation, and so forth (Connors, 1981). The curricula of Rose, Danziger, James, and others are dominated by some selection of these types of writing.

Teachers of this persuasion tend to devote little or no time to the procedures for the development of content. For Professor Rose, the learning of form is primary, and his assignments are designed to minimize substantive demands of writing in order to focus on a particular structure for organization. Once one knows the form, since meaning is directly apprehensible through the senses, content presents no problems; one may just look about at many examples and write.

In expressivist textbooks, "truth is conceived as the result of a private vision that must be constantly consulted in writing." Those who endorse this rhetoric "emphasize writing as a 'personal' activity, as an expression of one's unique voice" (Berlin, 1982, p. 772). Professor Green's commitment is precisely to this sort of rhetoric, to enabling students to reconstruct their own visions of what they "see" in the writing of others and of what they recall or reconstruct of their own experience. It is this view of truth as derivable from personal contemplation and interpretation that supports the focus on a single student at a time, as the student tells what he or she knows. It also leads to his abandoning other writing tasks (e.g., argument) and to relegating mechanics to independent work outside the classroom. Professor Green believes that if his teaching can help students see they have "something going" for themselves, that they have a voice that people find worth listening to, then they will have some reason to begin to clean up the little errors, and he contends that "repeatedly, they clean it up."

Berlin (1982) calls "new rhetoric" epistemic because it is a view of rhetoric "as a means of arriving at the truth" (p. 773). In the new rhetoric, he says:

> Truth is dynamic and dialectical, the result of a process involving the interaction of opposing elements. It is a relation that is created, not pre-existent and waiting to be discovered. . . . The New Rhetoric denies that truth is discoverable in sense impression since this data must always be interpreted—structured and organized—in order to have meaning. (p. 774)

Mr. Gow's commitment appears to be to a rhetoric of this kind. Although he stresses the need to observe carefully what is in the prints, his focus is on interpretation and learning the strategies that interpretation demands. He allows students to develop their own interpretations, to argue them, and to evaluate the interpretations of others. The understanding of the Hogarth engravings is not to be discovered but, instead, created through a dialectical process that involves the interactions of the students' ideas as they come to grips with their sense impressions by structuring and organizing them. He believes that learning to make the interpretation is essential to the writing tasks that constitute his goals. (Interestingly, although he asks students to compare and contrast images in the two engravings, he sees comparing and contrasting as tools of interpretation, strategies of inquiry, not simply a form for "expository writing.")

Although I have claimed that the teachers in our sample exhibit an epistemological stance, most appear to have adopted a stance without considering alternatives. Nearly all regard what they do as merely a means of teaching writing with no epistemological implications. (Mr. Gow is an exception. He specifies his belief that teachers cannot simply transplant their knowledge to the heads of students. Rather, students must construct their own knowledge through experience and in collaboration with others.) Rather than through considering alternatives and making a conscious choice, most teachers appear to have acquired the stance through what Lortie (1975) would call an "apprenticeship of observation" in schools, or through textbooks, or through association with other teachers.

If that is the case, it may help to explain the fact that several of the teachers who are primarily objectivist proponents of current traditional rhetoric also make use of episodes that must be classified as constructivist. That is, they devote a small but significant proportion of their time to activities involving the construction of knowledge concerned with form or substance: brainstorming, peer feedback about structure or content, group discussions of stories or other materials, and so forth. Four teachers, other than Professor Green, devote over 15% of their classroom time to such activities.

One of those displaying a mixed stance is Professor Kramer, who teaches the lowest level course of any teacher in the sample. In Chapter 7 we saw that Professor Kramer engaged her students in several constructive activities involving procedural knowledge. But we also saw her lecturing on nouns and pronouns as subjects, verbs, and the problems of agreement, followed by work sheets in which students were to identify subjects and verbs, activities that are clearly objectivist.

PRACTICAL LEARNING THEORY

None of the teachers in this sample refer to any standard learning theories, yet it is clear that underlying their work are what amount to relatively simple practical theories that enable teachers to order activities. In essence, many of the theories may be reduced to hypothetical statements of the if . . . then variety. For most of the objectivist teachers concerned with mechanics and usage, the statement may be extended to three parts: if I explicate the rules, and if students do appropriate exercises in applying the rules, then students should be able to use the convention appropriately in their writing. In nearly every case, an episode of lecture-recitation on a convention is followed by an episode consisting of one or more exercises in which students apply the rules governing the use of the convention. The origin of this practical theory appears to lie with the English grammar books of the 18th century, if not with the Latin grammars that were their predecessors (Hillocks & Smith, 1991).

A comparable theory appears to be held by objectivist teachers concerned with what I classified as formal discourse knowledge, the formal and rhetorical features of the types of writing taught. The if . . . then statement, again, commonly has three parts, as in the following: If I tell students the features of the type of writing (e.g., classification), and if I show them a model of such writing, they should be able to write the kind of product that I expect. We see this theory operating in Professor Rose's explanations of the five-paragraph theme and of classification and in Professor Kramer's explanations of the characteristics of a good paragraph. Professor James, who presents procedures for making evaluations, and in our classification is concerned with the substantive more than the formal, also follows this learning theory: If I explain how to make an evaluation and show students models of evaluation, then . . .

In my experience, this practical theory, which might be called the teacher-tells-and-students-do theory, is so deeply ingrained into the psyches of many English teachers that it makes the consideration of other possibilities next to impossible. It appears to be an integral part of teacher lore, "the accumulated body of traditions, practices, and beliefs in terms of which practitioners understand how writing is done, learned, and taught" (North, 1987, p. 22).

As North (1987) points out, this body of knowledge is not rigorous, but it is pragmatically logical, concerned with what is done, what might be done, and what might work. It has the characteristics of what Atran (1990) calls a folk theory, at least in the sense that it is egocentric, experiential, and partial. It focuses on what the teacher is to do, not on the results nor on the prediction of the results in any rigorous way. Such practical theories inform the teacher of what to do and provide assurance that having done those things, teaching has transpired. If the teacher has lectured on the uses of quotation marks and other conventions of the standard representation of dialogue and if he or she has required the students to do certain workbook exercises using those conventions, the teacher can assume that he or she has taught the punctuation of dialogue. There is little or no more to do, because the theory calls for no more.

Professor Dobbs provides a variation on these theories. He does lecture in great detail on standard usage. However, the exercises he includes are substantially different from the norm: that is, sentences to be corrected, usually with multiple-choice or fill-in-the-blank responses. Rather, Professor Dobbs's exercises are based on his idea that students need to practice something that they can, in his words, "do correctly" to the point of what he calls overlearning. However, the students do not know how to punctuate the materials that he dictates. They must navigate his "mispronunciations" so they may begin to see how speech must be used as a guide to the written word. In dictating them often enough, he believes, students will learn how to do it. He claims that this idea comes from coaching athletics, particularly basketball, where athletes practice dribbling, foul shooting, and so on, until they can do each flawlessly. He has argued by analogy to reach this practical learning theory to which he remains "firmly committed."

Both Mr. Gow and Professor Green manifest practical learning theories that differ markedly from those of the objectivists. Both believe that simply telling students what to do is inadequate, that students must experience doing the tasks that the writing demands, aided in a variety of ways. Both might tell students what to do, but both do much more. They create environments that will support the students as they engage in the strategies that the teacher presumes are required by the task. They each provide at least three kinds of support: introducing entry-level tasks for use of the target strategies, coaching as students engage in using the strategies, and presenting models of the kinds of writing sought.

Mr. Gow's entry-level task in preparation for interpreting the Hogarth engravings in groups is his initial teacher-led discussion of another, somewhat simpler engraving by Gilray. The students' engagement with the pieces by Hogarth is also supported by his coaching and the collaborative work of the students as they work in peer groups. Students' engagement with both Gilray and Hogarth provide support for later independent interpretation using comparable strategies with different material. In his interview, he also talks about the use of model compositions to help students see how they will write about their findings.

In Professor Green's classes, models of writing are much more important. In Chapter 6, we saw that some of these are professional and several are from students. He does not use them to analyze the structure of writing as do Professor Rose and several others. Rather, he uses the writings to prompt "recalls" of imagery, and he very carefully coaches students as they reconstruct the imagery as they have seen it in the mind's eye. The recalls are intended to exemplify the strategies students must use as they reconstruct the imagery of their own experience, and, in that respect, they practice doing what they will need to do independently. As Professor Green says, "It's permission, possibility, and model. It's the experience of it." His learning theory says that if he can coach students as they have the experience of using these procedures, they are likely to learn how to produce such imagery independently for this kind of empathic writing.

Clearly, the support he offers is quite different from Mr. Gow's collaborative peer-group work. Professor Green provides his coaching to one student at a time as the rest listen, assuming that all will gain insight into the strategies he coaches and emphasizing the necessity of listening to the personal voice. Mr. Gow, on the other hand, assumes that the interactive dialectic in the group work and in teacher-led discussions, along with his coaching, enables the learning.

The practical learning theories practiced by each teacher and outlined here are closely aligned to the rhetorical and epistemological stances they have adopted. The practical theory underlying Professor Green's work could be expressed as follows: "If I engage students in seeing the images of another's productions in their minds' eyes, and if I can help them to do the same with their own experience, translating both into words, then they should be able to do that whenever they write because the process provides model, permission, and opportunity." A key idea here lies in the phrase *if I can help them*. This phrase subsumes several subprocesses that include the necessity for the student to engage orally in the telling or recalling, the teacher's coaching as it progresses, and finally, the students' carrying through on the results individually. The idea of coaching requires an expansion as well. It requires some sort of model that sets a target for students to aim at, initial attempts by students to reach it, and interventions by the teacher to help them as they work.

Mr. Gow's practical theory is quite close to this. What students do in his groups becomes a model for inquiry, provides permission to use their own ideas, and gives the experience of engaging in the process of inquiry and developing an argument in support of an interpretation. His coaching requires a similar expansion. It requires that he invent an activity embedded in a context that allows students to engage in the process of inquiry. Without such engagement the process cannot take place.

Thus, the practical theories of both Gow and Green are essentially constructivist and are significantly different from those of the teachers who are essentially objectivist and see no need to invent a structure for engaging students prior to the teacher's giving information. This difference, I will argue, also involves a difference in pedagogical content knowledge.

CURRICULUM AND GOALS

We have studied teachers in college freshman writing programs and one high school English teacher. This fact alone suggests that we might encounter a somewhat restricted range of content and goals in the curriculum. However, even within the writing courses represented here, there remains a broad range of choices. Given the breadth of possibilities for inclusion in a writing course, selection is a necessity: no teacher could include everything possible. For the teachers in our study, the selection appears to be governed by a commitment to one of the four rhetorics, along with its epistemological and pedagogical stances, and to some view of the possible content or to some particular part of the content that provides an orientation for all the teaching that follows. And although we might say that all the teachers aim to teach writing, the specific goals concerning the types and features of writing to be taught vary extensively. Even within the group who adopt current traditional rhetoric we find wide variation in both goals and curricula. For example, several teach classification, definition, narrative, comparison and contrast, cause and effect, and so forth. Despite this common commitment, variation from teacher to teacher in both the macro- and microcurricula that students encounter is great. Clearly, each teacher constructs his or her own version of that rhetoric for classroom consumption. The difference between Professors James and Rose, for example, is very great (see Chapter 4). Another teacher ignores classification, definition, and other types included in the texts of current traditional rhetoric, and focuses on writing analyses of short stories. Professor Danziger combines descriptive writing with teaching sentence expansion using absolute phrases, the elimination of passives, and models from the Bulwer-Lytton contest and other sources in a way unique in this sample (see Chapter 2). A few teachers focus almost exclusively on the production of error-free prose, a commitment that appears to rely heavily on a building-block conception of curriculum that assumes students must master the mechanics of punctuating individual sentences before they proceed to writing their own sentences.

Certain of these commitments appear to be idiosyncratic. Professor Dobbs's commitment is to teaching mechanics up to a level of automaticity that he believes will enable students to produce the error-free prose required of them in college. Professor Rose has a commitment to his own special version of current-traditional rhetoric, certain types of exposition modified by his idea of the five-paragraph theme and his tripartite assignments. He believes that this structure is fundamental to any college writing assignment.

Even though these teachers have committed themselves to current traditional rhetoric, and even though their classroom processes have much in common, the episode-to-episode content of their curricula differs widely. The evidence is clear that they do not simply draw upon some common body of curricular knowledge, as Grossman (1990) appears to assume that teachers do. Rather, the evidence suggests that they construct their own versions of the curriculum from the body of knowledge that they have acquired over their years of teaching and from sources outside their teaching. Most teachers would not select passages from the Bulwer-Lytton contest, parodies of heavily laden description, as models for imitation. When Professor Danziger presents the passages, he smiles and tells his students that this is "marvelous, marvelous writing." He knows full well it is parody, but, at the same time, he hopes that his students will see the point of including more effective imagery in their own skeletal narratives. At the same time, he connects this to the use of absolute phrases, one of the few grammatical structures, the use of which has been correlated with gains in quality scores of writing (Hillocks, 1986). Professor Danziger has invented this sequence.

Professor James uses an early edition of the Axelrod and Cooper (1991) text, but the text does not control his course content. It is a supplement. Professor Dobbs invents a process for teaching correctness that is based on his ideas about coaching athletics. Examples could be readily proliferated to show that each teacher among those committed to current traditional rhetoric constructs his or her own curricula.

Underlying these differences are clear differences in goals, whether articulated or not. Danziger wants to improve descriptive writing, and although other teachers share this general goal, his subgoals (or criteria for judging improvement) apparently include using absolute phrases, eliminating passives, making use of detailed imagery, and so forth. Professor Dobbs's goals include not simply the elimination of error, but automaticity in eliminating it. No other teacher in the sample shares that dimension of the goal. Professor Rose drives for a particular version of the five-paragraph theme that no other teacher shares. Professor Kramer focuses on writing a "good paragraph," defined in the usual way as one having a thesis statement supported by detail. However, she incorporates instruction in the processes of writing and is concerned that her students build their confidence as writers. Other instructors focus on the paragraph but they do not include work on the prewriting, revision, peer feedback, and other process-oriented goals.

EPISTEMOLOGICAL STANCE AND CURRICULUM

Although many teachers are committed to current traditional rhetoric, which appears to entail an objectivist epistemological stance in their teaching, they, themselves, reconstruct the knowledge of their adopted rhetoric according to their own lights. That is, these teachers (for example, Danziger, Dobbs, James, Kramer, Rose, and Thomas) clearly construct their own curricula and goals for their own use in classrooms. Yet, by and large, they have adopted an objectivist epistemological stance for their classroom practice of lecture-recitation. They assume that their students will learn through the explanations of experts. As a result, they devote little class time to procedural knowledge, a process that necessarily engages students in the construction of their own developing knowledge.

Professor Green's commitment is based on an expressivist rhetoric, which emphasizes the development of a unique voice in writing. Knowing that, we would expect his classroom to be different from those of the other teachers in the sample.

One of the major differences is his emphasis on procedural knowledge, as he engages different class members in recalling what is read and in their own experience. Another appears to be his emphasis on narrative writing as a basis for all other kinds of writing. He believes that comparable teaching techniques will work with argument and other kinds of writing once the students come to enjoy writing and see themselves as capable writers.

Although we have no one else with whom to compare Green, an examination of his classes indicates that he too constructs the curriculum and its events even as they are in progress. But his constructions are dependent on those of his students. Thus he reads their writing and uses it to prompt recalls. When students recall and detail their own experiences in class, he coaches them to produce examples of the kind of writing that he wants them to produce. In essence, he is inventing at every step.

Mr. Gow also engages students in tasks that are intended to help them construct their own processes and knowledge, which they will eventually use independently. He claims to focus on several kinds of writing tasks, including personal narrative, drama, and several kinds of argument, especially arguments of interpretation and policy. He claims that he does not deal with expository writing because, he says, "as soon as you're concerned about other interpretations, you're going to be arguing, whether you're writing about what happened, what something means, or telling a good way to do something." Of personal narrative, he says, "Even when you're writing about your own experience, the details you include involve an interpretation of that experience. It's kind of an argument when you think about it." Such comments reflect Mr. Gow's epistemological stance, which I have classified as new or epistemic rhetoric because of its reliance on dialectic and bringing various student perspectives to bear on a problem, perspectives that result in the development of thoughtful arguments.

That stance results in classroom activities different from Professor Green's. Whereas Green concentrates on one student at a time, Gow focuses on engaging students with others so that they may disagree and learn from each other's perceptions and interpretations. This is precisely what we would expect of someone adopting Berlin's (1982) "new rhetoric."

Mr. Gow clearly invents the idea for the lesson presented in Chapter 1. However, although he knows in advance that he will lead a discussion of one engraving and ask students to discuss the Hogarth engravings in small groups prior to a class discussion of their findings, the content of the discussions is dependent at each step on the constructions of the students, guided, to some extent, by his coaching. His own contributions depend on the constructions of his students. In short, much of the microcurricula in both the Green and Gow classrooms are co-constructed.

Clearly, in the group of teachers we studied, the curricula cannot be represented as a body of preexisting knowledge, except in the most general sense.

Teachers transform even that general body of knowledge for their own use. Both curricula and goals are clearly influenced by a teacher's epistemological-rhetorical stance.

CONCEPTIONS OF STUDENTS AND CURRICULUM

We have seen that teachers in this sample have different expectations of their students. Although each college has a system for placing students in English 98, 100, or 101, teachers' attitudes about their students are not dependent on that classification. Thus Professor Kramer, who teaches English 98, is more positive in her outlook than is Professor Rose, who teaches 101. Professor Green, teaching 100, is more positive than is Professor Dobbs, who teaches the same level. These differing beliefs about students' capabilities are not based on preexisting classifications, but are constructions by the teacher based on the students' perceived responses to instruction. Thus, Rose says, "No matter what I do, there is only minimal improvement." Green, on the other hand, talks about how strong his students' writing is and how much they do. He requires 80 typewritten pages per semester but claims that his students do much more than that.

These constructions of students and their abilities have a profound effect on the construction of curricula. I have already argued that when teacher expectations for students are low, the goals of instruction become restricted through simplification. This simplification may take place through a variety of processes, notable among which are reduction, fragmentation, and what Bereiter and Scardamalia (1987) refer to as substantive facilitation. By reduction, I mean simplifying the task to a point that it no longer represents an authentic real-world task. Professor Rose reduces the discourse knowledge he teaches to the five-paragraph theme and adapts assignments so that the content and its treatment are also simplified through the tripartite structure he assigns. Substantive facilitation occurs when a teacher simply tells a student how to punctuate a specific sentence or what to say. Professor Rose, for example, uses this process when he explicates the content that should appear in Horace's writing.

Fragmentation appears when the teacher emphasizes some part of a writing task without integrating it into the whole. A focus on mechanics or the paragraph are examples. Professor Dobbs fragments writing instruction when he concentrates for long stretches of time on asking students to punctuate the same passages that he dictates several times. He excludes actual writing until the final 4 weeks of the semester, when he asks students to write only the simplest informative narratives: "Write about what you had for breakfast this morning, or write about something that happened on the way to school." He fragments intentionally, so that students will not have to process complex content and, at the same time, worry about the punctuation.

In contrast to Professor Rose stands Professor James, who has high expecta-tions of his students and has planned his course to move from relatively simple pieces of writing to much more complex pieces. Even his simple tasks are legiti-mate and authentic writing tasks. Further, James concentrates on explaining the procedures for the intellectual task essential to the assignment, for example, an evaluation. He does not require the simplified five-paragraph theme, nor does he restrict the shape of the writing in other ways. Professor James does not tell stu-dents what the content should be at any stage, only the strategies that they should use. But unlike Mr. Gow, he does not use classroom time to engage them in using the strategies involved.

In similar ways, Professor Kramer, who has relatively high expectations for her students in a lower level course stands in contrast to Professor Dobbs. First, even though she fragments the writing by her focus on the paragraph, she engages students in actual writing from the beginning of the course and attempts to en-gage them in brainstorming for ideas, instead of merely explaining what the con-tent should be, as does Professor Rose. Second, her requirements for writing are more complex than those of Professor Dobbs. She asks students to write pieces in support of opinions, for example, instead of simple reports of experience. In addi-tion, she engages them in small collaborative group work to revise and edit their own work.

Both Mr. Gow and Professor Green believe that their students can learn very complex strategies for writing, if they approach teaching the strategies in an appro-priate way. The data available in this study does not permit a strong argument concerning the relationship between positive beliefs about students and episte-mological stance. However, it seems logical to assume that a constructivist stance would not be acceptable to a teacher who believed that his or her students were incapable of responding positively to the kinds of activities we find in the two constructivist classrooms. At the same time, the objectivist stance appears to be highly compatible with the assumption that students are weak. For example, many calls to teach the basics are really calls for simple declarative knowledge.

In short, in this sample at least, what teachers believe students are able to do has a clear impact not only on the goals and purposes they adopt, but also on the microcurricula, the minute-to-minute and day-to-day activities they develop for their students.

PEDAGOGICAL CONTENT KNOWLEDGE

Like most other areas of teacher knowledge, pedagogical content knowledge ap-pears not to be some body of preexisting knowledge that teachers dip into, but knowledge constructed by the teacher in light of the teacher's epistemological stance and conceptions of knowledge to be taught (in this case rhetoric or writing), learning theory, and students. The most important of these appears to be the epistemological stance.

Shulman (1987) has stated that pedagogical content knowledge is not necessarily shared by persons having the same content knowledge. That is, whereas literary scholars and high school teachers may have the same content knowledge concerning a literary work and its interpretations, a skilled high school teacher is likely to have quite different knowledge about how to teach that work. For Shulman, this knowledge is not simply different but unique. McEwan and Bull (1991) challenge this distinction, expressing concern "that [Shulman's] distinction between content knowledge and pedagogical content knowledge introduces an unnecessary and untenable complication into the conceptual framework." They argue that "all content knowledge, whether held by scholars or teachers, has a pedagogical dimension" (p. 318). This is an important dispute for one major reason. If pedagogical content knowledge is not unique, then it may be learned by virtue of learning appropriate content knowledge. If it is not unique, then teacher education ought to focus on content knowledge, as many advocate. McEwan and Bull see Shulman as making the following claim:

> Teachers need to be concerned about whether their representations of subject matter are teachable to others; scholars, by implication, do not. (p. 319)

They go on to ask:

> Why should scholars' representations be privileged in comparison with teachers' representations? And why should the teachability of representations be of no concern to scholars? Shulman never directly answers these questions, but one natural answer immediately suggests itself: because scholars' representations are an accurate representation of the world as it really is; they are objectively true. (p. 319)

These are interesting questions, but surely more than one "natural answer . . . suggests itself." Another possibility is that scholars do not have to make special efforts to communicate with those who know nothing of their fields, and further, they can afford to assume that their peers have enough knowledge to understand verbal representations of their work. Teachers in general and in this sample do not make that assumption. Most go to pains to clarify their explanations so that students will understand what they have to say. Still, to the extent that teachers make explanations, their pedagogical content knowledge is not different in kind from that of scholars. It is representational. But several teachers in this sample go beyond providing representations of subject matter.

McEwan and Bull (1991) further assert that Shulman and his students claim that "Dewey's account of subject matter supports the case for its [subject matter's] division into scholarly and pedagogic forms" (p. 325). McEwan and Bull, of course, argue that it does not. They argue that no transformation of subject matter is necessary in Dewey's account of teaching, rather "only transformation of the world in which students act." They emphasize Dewey's idea that subject matter ought not influence instruction directly, but rather influence how "teachers create activities and organize the learning environment." In Dewey's view, they continue:

> Subject matter enters into the calculations of teaching only as an endpoint—a map or formulated statement of experience that summarizes the results of previous experiences. . . . Teachers must be confident that what they get students to do will *finally* lead them to a knowledge of organized subject matter. . . . Thus, no transformation of the subject matter is ever required in Dewey's picture of teaching, *only transformation of the world in which students act.* (p. 329; italics mine)

Only transformation of the world in which students act? This is exactly the key difference between the knowledge of scholars and the knowledge of teachers. Scholars are particularly concerned with the presentation of the declarative knowledge of content in books and articles. To some extent teachers share this concern. But in addition, teachers must convey procedural knowledge to students who are not initiates, who do not already have most of the procedures for achieving certain ends. For this purpose, they seek "transformation of the world in which students act."

How are such activities different from representations of knowledge? The knowledge involved is not declarative. It is usually procedural, knowledge of the type that Ryle (1984) refers to as knowledge in performance. It is knowledge of how to do something. The knowledge that scholars represent for others is almost always declarative, a verbal or symbolic representation. Even when a scholar wants to impart a procedure, it is imparted by way of verbal or other symbolic maps. Skilled teachers may provide such maps, but in addition, they organize activities through which students learn what is to be learned through active participation.

Such invention is highly complex (Hillocks, 1995). It appears to be standard for Gow and Green and appears less often in the work of other teachers. In this sample, the objectivist teachers attempt to convey declarative knowledge during most of their instructional time. However, even among this group, not all activity is representational. Professor Thomas's group discussion of Jane's composition is not essentially representational, even though most of her teaching involves lecture (see Chapter 4). The small group transforms the environment in such a way that Jane comes to see the problem herself. Professor Kramer's use of group work and such activities as brainstorming are not aimed at conveying knowledge, but at helping students develop it. Transformations of environments are the norm in a variety of sources (Troyka, 1973; Kahn, Johannessen, & Walter, 1984; Lee, 1993; Stern, 1995).

When teachers provide explanations or representations of subject matter, their knowledge is different only in degree from that of scholars. But when they set up the paths to knowledge in their classroom activities, the knowledge they use is different in kind from that of scholars. It is precisely this *"transformation of the world in which students act"* (McEwan & Bull, 1991, p. 329, italics mine) that makes pedagogical content knowledge unique and powerful.

At the heart of such transformations lies reflection of the highest order, reflection that involves knowledge of the students and what they can do, detailed knowledge of the learning task that is the goal, an openness to the myriad of possibilities that might make the desired learning possible, and an ability to imagine and evaluate what the consequences of any set of activities might be.

Mr. Gow makes the process sound easy, but we have only his retrospective account. He says,

> I don't really know how I came up with them (the Hogarth engravings). I thought about the activity for a long time. I thought about using ads, but, you know, they're too simple. There's no disagreement. I thought about using short films, but that's a pain. . . . You lose a lot of time. I wanted something that would get attention right away and that would demand interpretation. Anyway, I thought of these. And at first, I wasn't sure if they were too complex. So I tried them on my own kids, who are a bit younger. Bingo! They were fascinated, especially with *Gin Lane*. So that was that. I decided to try them. I'll use them again.

What we need is a protocol of the invention sequence, but that may not be easy to collect. Mr. Gow adds that he thought of the Hogarth engravings in the shower.

CONCLUSIONS ABOUT TEACHER THINKING

All of this provides the basis for several conclusions about teacher knowledge. First, although Shulman (1987) outlines seven categories of teacher knowledge, five of these appear to be primarily responsible for what happens in classes: general subject matter knowledge, general learning theory, knowledge of students, knowledge of curriculum, and pedagogical content knowledge. The two remaining categories are simply not salient in the data of this study. No doubt our teachers have knowledge of the contexts in which their teaching takes place, but it does not appear to be a major determinant of their thinking and practice. Teachers in this study are not cognizant of formal learning theories. The case may be different with elementary and secondary school teachers, because they have taken the courses that the education establishment believes will familiarize them with learning theories. The one secondary school teacher in this study, Mr. Gow, does not refer to learning theories, however. In my experience, secondary school teachers do not operate on the basis of formal learning theories. What counts for them is their apprenticeships of observation (Lortie, 1975), through which they have developed their own practical theories of learning and teaching.

Second, these categories of knowledge do not exist as repositories of knowledge from which teachers borrow. Nor do they exist simply as stories, as Bruner (1985), Elbaz (1983), and Clandinin and Connelly (1995) suggest. Rather, they are constructed by each teacher and are influenced by the teacher's life experience and appear to exist as arguments. That is, teachers, in explaining why they teach what they teach, put their responses in the form of simple arguments complete with claims, evidence, warrants, qualifications, and sometimes rebuttals.

Third, the categories of knowledge do not exist as independent entities from which teachers select in the design of their micro- and macrocurricula. Rather, they interact strongly, influencing teaching processes and probably outcomes.

Fourth, although epistemological stance has not previously been considered to be involved in teaching processes, this study suggests that it must be considered in conjunction with the categories if we are to understand more completely how teacher knowledge impacts on classroom practice. It appears to be a powerful influence on the construction teacher knowledge.

Finally, the nature of reflective practice is strongly shaped by the practical theories at work, the constructed categories underlying them, and a teacher's epistemological stance.

TEACHER KNOWLEDGE AND IDENTITY

The knowledge and commitments of the teachers in this sample strongly influence their teaching identity. We do not find that Professor Dobbs will teach as Professor Green does on one day and as Professor James does on another. Nor does his course begin to look like Professor Kramer's. For the most part, teachers seem to say, "This is what my students are like. This is what is important to teach, and this is how I teach it." And that carries them into the future. Although there are some changes from one year's observations to the next, each teacher substantially retains the teaching identity established on the basis of his or her constructed knowledge of students, goals, curricula, pedagogical content knowledge, rhetoric, and epistemological stance.

In our study, we have seen no teacher make substantial revisions in teaching while a class is in progress. Some teachers, however, have talked about changes in their planning, changes that may call for the use of new assignments or revisions of old ones (Professor James), the use of ideas picked up from a newspaper (Professor Wade), a change in textbooks and the incorporation of journal writing for the first few minutes of each class (Professor Ballard), or the use of new materials as an introduction to specific learning as in Mr. Gow's classes.

These changes are deliberated and are the product of some dissatisfaction with what had been used previously. The teacher in effect says, "Gosh, that did not work well. How can I do this better?" Professor James does just this with his *Modest Proposal* assignment when he recognizes that it does not work very well. However, among the teachers who are not optimistic about their students' ability to learn, we find little activity of this kind. These teachers tend to present either what they regard as basic skills training (Professor Dobbs) or relatively simple formulas for writing (Professor Rose) or both.

In short, the cluster of knowledge that the teacher garners over a career appears to remain stable. If teachers change in dramatic ways, this brief 2-year study could not identify the changes. After the conclusion of the data collection, three teachers told me of a metamorphosis. But the data available does not cover the time in which change occurred. Still, it may be that understanding teacher knowledge will permit greater change. After teaching in various institutions for over 40 years, I can remember witnessing few dramatic changes.

This is not a very optimistic view of teacher knowledge. On the other hand, this study suggests that if attitudes or epistemological stance were to change, perhaps other parts of teacher knowledge would also change.

❧ 8 ❧

Implications

WHAT ARE THE IMPLICATIONS of this conception of teacher knowledge for practice, preservice teacher education, and research? If the model of teacher knowledge enunciated in Chapter 7 has some reasonable level of validity, we are left with several questions about teacher change, preservice education, and research:

1. What does the model predict about the nature and effects of efforts to reform teaching?
2. What does the model suggest about the nature of preservice education programs?
3. What other research will be useful for testing the model and gaining further insight into the impact of teacher knowledge on practice?

Embedded in each of these is a host of other questions. I will approach them in order, beginning with the problem of teacher change. To examine this important question, it will be necessary to turn first to the question of how teacher knowledge affects reflective practice.

TEACHER CHANGE AND REFLECTIVE PRACTICE

In Chapter 7, I argued that the construct that makes up what an individual teacher knows is highly stable, with changes coming, if at all, in relatively small things, perhaps the addition of occasional group work and, therefore, less lecture-recitation; perhaps a new writing assignment; or perhaps a new idea to include in a lecture on punctuating dialogue. Since people are unlikely to change unless they see a clear need, we need to ask what it is that enables such insight. The answer, I think, is reflective practice. Therefore, I will turn first to a definition of reflective practice and, second, to an analysis of how teacher knowledge may promote or retard reflective practice.

Reflective Practice

Fenstermacher (1994), in his review of the epistemological dimensions of research on teacher thinking, classifies the work of Schön (1987) on reflective practice as part of the question about what teachers know. Reflection in practice, as defined by Dewey and Schön, certainly has to do with content and content-related pedagogical knowledge. McEwan and Bull (1991) summarize Dewey's ideas on reflective activity in teaching and scholarship to show that what the teacher does, at least in this arena, has much in common with what the scholar does. Whereas the scholar, they say, is guided by hypotheses, the teacher is guided by "organized subject matter":

> Thus, hypotheses and subject matter are part of a developing system of knowledge. These leading ideas guide the actions of teachers and scholars. They lead the scholar to experiment and the teacher to the construction of educational activities. As a next step, the consequences of these activities must be observed and the results reviewed. Reflection on these processes produces new learning. (p. 330)

This position is in harmony with Donald Schön's (1987) ideas about reflective practice, the difference being that Schön is concerned with what he calls reflection in action, a kind of research and experiment that are embedded in action and that may not have the full range of ratiocinative antecedents that research has. That is, when action is required, the practitioner acts on the basis of what he or she knows but without separating the intellectual from the practical. Schön puts it this way:

> Although we sometimes think before acting, it is also true that in much of the spontaneous behavior of skillful practice we reveal a kind of knowing which does not stem from a prior intellectual operation. (p. 50)

In a situation of practice, we act on what we believe to be desirable and what we think are the means for bringing about the desirable end, but without necessarily thinking each of these through as we might at a time when action is not immediately demanded. For Schön, practice differs from research in other ways, all of which have to do with the relationship between changing things and understanding them:

> The practitioner has an interest in transforming the situation from what it is to something he likes better. He also has an interest in understanding the situation, but it is in the service of his interest in change. (p. 147)

Schön (1987) also distinguishes between reflective practice and what he calls the idea of technical rationality, the kind of knowledge that we use in finding the area of a circle or in following the directions in a manual to set up new electronic equipment. In teaching, the problems we confront are not amenable to such simple solutions, because the problems themselves are fuzzy, likely to be characterized by, in Schön's words, "uncertainty, instability, uniqueness, and value conflict" (p. 49). To deal with such a problem, practitioners frame it, or construct it. Schön puts it this way:

> When we set the problem, we select what we will treat as the "things" of the situation, we set the boundaries of our attention to it, and we impose upon it a coherence which allows us to say what is wrong and in what directions the situation needs to be changed. Problem setting is a process in which, interactively, we *name* the things to which we will attend and *frame* the context in which we will attend to them. (p. 40)

In Clark and Peterson (1986), a teacher comments that her explanation to students was not very clear. In doing so, she brings together her thinking about the subject, the objective of her explanation, the character of that explanation, and the child's comprehension of it. That very unification allows her to decide what to do to make it clearer, without "ratiocinating" her way to a decision, and she can put it into action even as she thinks it.

According to Schön (1987), when the process of reflection-in-action goes well, the practitioner interacts with the situation in such a way that it talks back to the practitioner. That is to say, as the practitioner makes a move in the existing situation, it changes, in a sense "talking back" to the practitioner, such that each shapes the other. When the process goes well,

> this conversation with the situation is reflective. In answer to the situation's back-talk, the [practitioner] reflects-in-action on the construction of the problem, the strategies of action, or the model of the phenomena, which have been implicit in his moves. (p. 79)

This continuing interactive experiment is made possible by the practitioner's evaluation of the unfolding events of the process: a continuing evaluation of his or her moves in terms of their results, their conformity with earlier goals and moves, and new problems that arise. We might say that the teacher has a subject matter goal or image that serves as a template against which he or she may judge the impact of each move in light of the context in which the former move was made. Thus each ensuing move by the teacher is made in a new context brought by the interaction of the accumulation of teacher moves in combination with student responses.

This implies that skilled teachers continually monitor what is happening in their classrooms. Teachers such as Professors Green, Kramer, and Thomas and Mr. Gow appear to monitor what happens, compare it to some conception of what they hope will happen, and either intervene to help students move in the direction of the goal or reformulate the goal and allow students to proceed.

Mr. Gow, for example, notes that one small group appears to have focused on the simple comparison of alcohol consumption in the two engravings and have not considered the pawnbroker buildings in either *Gin Lane* or *Beer Street*. He says, "Have you thought about these two buildings (pointing)? Do you know what those signs are?" A boy knows that they are pawnbroker signs. "Think about why those buildings are there." As students begin to compare the buildings and their function in the two pictures, Mr. Gow passes to another group. When he hears students comparing the tools and signs of trade that the people in *Beer Street* carry, he is surprised because he himself had not thought of that. However, he recognizes their importance and reformulates his goal regarding the interpretation. In effect, he has learned from his students.

In planning and teaching, we can think of the frame experiment as having five major contextual components: students and our knowledge of their past performance, interests, proclivities, and so on; the trial event, which may be thought of as a single move such as a question or a sequence of events over a day or several weeks; a specific goal for the particular students involved, but understood within the context of an array of educational goals; responses of the students; and the curricular context of the event. This formulation of reflective practice, however, indicates the limitations of reflective practice by the very components that make it possible. To some extent or other, the frames that teachers set necessarily depend upon the knowledge they bring to them. Thus, reflection is necessarily limited by the nature of teacher knowledge.

The limits are set by the practical theories generated by the teacher's epistemological stance and attitudes toward students. In the section on learning theory included in Chapter 7, I defined these practical theories as hypothetical statements of the if . . . then variety. One of Professor James's theories might be stated as follows: If I explain how to evaluate in detail, and if I show students models of successful evaluations, then my students will be able to write their own evaluations. Such practical theories appear to interact with optimistic or nonoptimistic beliefs about students. That is, if a teacher believes that students are able and likely to learn, students' failure is likely to be a surprise to the teacher and to trigger questions about the teaching. If, on the other hand, teachers believe that students are unlikely to do well, there will be little surprise if they fail and little reason to question the effectiveness of teaching. Whether reflection takes place in preteaching, teaching, or postteaching, the same strictures hold.

Schön's (1987) concern is with reflection-in-action, which he sees as involving a conversation between the practitioner and the situation, made possible by "back-talk" from the situation. This conversation is at the heart of reflection-in-action. In teaching, the main back-talk from the situation comes in the form of students' responses. Objectivist teachers, however, by their mode of operation (lecture-recitation, seat work on restricted exercises, and so forth) minimize the possibilities for back-talk from the situation. Even when student response is available, objectivist teachers may ignore the possibility for evaluation because they assume that the knowledge they provide is directly apprehensible. For example, when Professor Kramer is teaching subject-verb agreement, she explains that to decide on the correct verb, students will first have to identify the subject of the sentence:

> PROFESSOR KRAMER: Before we decide whether we're going to use the singular or the plural verb, we've got to know what the subject is. And remember that *here* cannot be the subject. Why, because *here* is not a noun or a pronoun. And a subject has to be either a noun or a pronoun. Which part of speech would *here* and *there* be, do you know? Anyone?
>
> LISA: *Here* is present.
>
> PROFESSOR KRAMER: *Here, there?*
>
> REUBEN: It's an adjective.
>
> PROFESSOR KRAMER: No, it's an adverb. They're what we call adverbs.
>
> STUDENTS: Oh, adverbs.
>
> PROFESSOR KRAMER: They're actually adverbs of place. *Here, there, everywhere,* they're adverbs of place. And the subject cannot be an adverb. The subject has to be either a noun or a pronoun. So if you begin a sentence with here or there, that's not the subject. You've got to look elsewhere for the subject. Let's finish the sentence. *Here is or are a new book.* What's the subject of the sentence?
>
> ALICE: New?
>
> LORENZO: Book.
>
> PROFESSOR KRAMER: *Book* is the subject. You're right. That's what we're talking about is this subject. So even though it's the last word in the sentence, it's the subject. Nobody ever said that the subject has to come at the beginning of the sentence. Usually it does, but it doesn't have to. The subject could even be the last word in the whole sentence. Now, let's turn the sentence around. And that will tell us which verb to use. What the sentence really means is, *a new book is here.* (Students echo her) OK? Let's finish the next sentence. *There was or were five students absent.*
>
> LORENZO: Was.
>
> PROFESSOR KRAMER: Subject?
>
> LORENZO: *Students.*
>
> PROFESSOR KRAMER: *Students* is the subject. You're right, but it's plural. And therefore we've got to use the plural verb *were.*

These students are faced with a kind of double whammy. Even when they do correctly identify the subject, they may not be able to identify the verb appropriate to standard usage. In Lorenzo's big-city dialect the expression *there was five students* is perfectly acceptable.

The effectiveness of such a presentation of declarative knowledge must be judged upon students' abilities to recognize the subject of sentences and to recognize the appropriate match between subject and verb. The transcript suggests that students do not recognize subjects and do not recognize the appropriate match between subject and verb to effect the agreement called for in standard English. However, the teacher does not seem to perceive that her elaborate explanations have not worked very well. If she has, she makes no move to change the method of teaching, apparently assuming that the necessary rules can be learned if she explains often enough. This assumption appears to be an effect of her objectivist stance, which allows few opportunities for response, all of which appear to be guesses at the right answer.

Constructivist teachers, on the other hand, maximize the possibilities for response by using activities that engender high levels of student response. In fact, as argued earlier, student response is a necessary part of the practical theory involved. Both Gow and Green plan for response upon which to build. They listen intently to what their students have to say in order to shape the emerging knowledge that students are constructing. When students are off target, they find ways to bring them back through suggestions and questions. As we have seen, they construct knowledge together with their students.

Profiles of Reflective Practice

This analysis suggests at least three general profiles of reflective practice. The first is founded on a combination of a constructive epistemological stance and optimism about students' abilities to learn, and has, in effect, appeared in the descriptions of the classes of Mr. Gow and Professor Green. Earlier, I suggested that reflective moments occur within frames that have five dimensions: knowledge of students, a specific goal for students, the trial event, student responses, and the curricular context in which the event occurs. If we think of Mr. Gow's work on the Hogarth engravings as an event, we can outline a frame for reflective practice as follows:

- *Knowledge of students.* Students are capable and able to deal with complex tasks with appropriate aid.
- *Specific goal.* To interpret the engravings in order to understand Hogarth's point.
- *Trial event.* Groups work collaboratively on an initial interpretation.
- *Student responses.* Students talk about the consumption of alcohol in both engravings but ignore the contrasting pawnbroker shops.

- *Curricular context.* Sequence leading to independent development and defense of interpretations in writing.

Mr. Gow knows where he hopes the current activity will lead: to independent development and defense of interpretations in writing. The specific activity is an early step in that direction. When Mr. Gow notes that the students are focusing on the consumption of alcohol but ignoring the pawnbroker shops, which are prominent in both *Beer Street* and *Gin Lane*, he realizes that they are ignoring a large part of the data that they must interpret. Therefore, he calls their attention to them. However, he does not tell students how to make the interpretation. His faith in them leads him to believe that simply pointing out the problem will lead them to their own solution. Therefore, he simply says, "Have you thought about these two buildings (pointing)? Do you know what those signs are?" When a boy says that they are pawnbroker signs, he adds, "Think about why those buildings are there." He does not simply supply a correct answer, as does Professor Kramer.

Because optimistic teachers such as Mr. Gow assume that students will learn under appropriate circumstances, and because they understand that students must be engaged in the construction of their own knowledge, they set about developing activities that will allow students to do just that. Because their activities allow students to respond frequently in class to a variety of factors, they are also privy to what students are doing in response to the activity and what they seem to be thinking. Given this openness, such teachers are able to evaluate progress, consider possible revisions in the activity or the store of ideas available, and take action to facilitate change in their students even while they work.

A different profile emerges when the teacher is both objectivist and not optimistic about what students will learn. These teachers seem to believe that students either have the wherewithal to do the work required or they do not. They believe that their own students are not prepared, but they do not preclude the possibility that other students may be quite capable of meeting their standards. However, they do not expect that their students are likely to succeed. This perception of the students' weaknesses governs instruction. No teacher in this group describes teaching "better" students differently. They apparently aim their teaching at the students whom they assume will not do well—in each case, the whole group.

In this profile the most important assumption about the nature of teaching is that it is tantamount to telling. If one tells or gives students appropriate information, it will be up to students to learn it. The telling may take place through a textbook, a lecture, or as teacher-led discussions that amount to recitations, although teachers invariably call these, and sometimes their lectures, discussion.

Teachers in this profile treat their assumptions about students as axiomatic. Because they perceive students as having very weak backgrounds, they adopt the corollary that whatever is taught must be simplified and "highly structured." The simplification and "structure" should enable teachers to "transfuse" the necessary information directly into the minds of their students. One teacher in this profile, for example, believes that because his students cannot think for themselves, they "want to be force-fed." He says, "The more structure they have, the more comfortable they are with an assignment." Certainly, all teachers simplify, introducing the simplest version of difficult concepts first. These are often skeletal at first, later taking on the flesh and sinew of far more complex ideas. In this profile, however, the simplified version is the goal. One teacher in this profile, for example, will not allow students to write more than a paragraph, because "they have so much trouble developing a good paragraph."

Another teacher simplifies teaching subject-verb agreement in the third-person singular with what he calls "the rule of one *s*." This rule holds that if the subject ends in *s*, the verb does not, and vice versa. Curiously, if this is a rule for proofreaders, as it appears to be, the problems with it are apparent. First, if an *s* appears on both, there is no way, from the rule, to make a decision about which to delete. Second, if it appears on neither, as is the case in some dialects of English, there is no way to decide where to add the *s*. If, on the other hand, it is a rule for generating text, there is no way to decide which of the two receives an *s* in the first place. Similar formulaic simplification appears in the teaching of discourse structures, for example, the five-paragraph theme.

The two basic assumptions about students and teaching in this profile, taken together with their corollaries, form a very tight syllogistic system for thinking about teaching. Because the students are weak, they cannot be expected to learn very much. Therefore, they require simplified formulas and are likely to have difficulty even with them. Since most of the teaching is presentational, and since there is little response from students during class time, the possibilities for reflection on student understandings are highly restricted.

Further, the conception of teaching allows for a very straightforward method of evaluating teaching: if the proper formulas about writing have been presented, then proper teaching has taken place. If, then, students do not learn much even when proper teaching has taken place, it is not surprising because they are weak and cannot be expected to learn. In short, the basic assumptions are such that they entail the conclusions. Teaching writing under these assumptions becomes a protected activity. There is no need to call assumptions or methods into question, no need to try something new, no reason to doubt one's teaching methods.

The third profile includes a large number of teachers who are primarily objectivist but are also optimistic about their students and who sometimes use constructivist activities. During constructivist activities, they appear to be reflective in action. But during their objectivist operations, they seem not to be. Witness Professor Kramer's treatment of subject and verbs above. At the same time, the members of this group do appear to make changes in their course plans on the basis of what they observe to be the results of their teaching. Several of these teachers, for example, had recently opted to use different texts because they felt that they would be more effective. My guess is that these teachers who show a mixed stance are more open to change than are those in the preceding profile.

IMPLICATIONS FOR TEACHER CHANGE

If the conclusions laid out above are solidly based, and I believe they are, they hold serious implications for teacher change. First, the kinds of teaching that this study finds most often (lecture and recitation) is very common at all levels of education (Goodlad, 1984; Hoetker & Ahlbrand, 1969; and Nystrand et al., 1997). Second, recent research strongly indicates that such teaching is largely ineffective. Hillocks (1986), for example, finds that the kind of teaching in Mr. Gow's classroom results in student gains several times greater than those of students in lecture-recitation classes. Nystrand et al. (1997) have a similar finding for literature learning. Third, the findings here suggest that teacher change will come with far more difficulty than anyone may have expected.

Change will be a matter of far more than learning new methods of teaching or instituting a new curriculum for teachers to follow. Teachers who have adopted an objectivist stance and who are not optimistic about their students will have no reason to change. Because they so seldom engage in reflective practice, they will have little evidence of any need to change. And because they have low expectations of their students, they will not be surprised when their students fail to learn. They know, by their own lights, that there is no need to change. They are usually confident that if anything would succeed with their students, their methods would. After all, in their minds, they have made what is to be learned as simple as possible, and their students still have not learned very well.

For the past 3 years, I have been working on a study of the impact of state mandatory writing assessments on policy and practice at the school district and school levels. As part of that study, my colleagues and I have interviewed teachers at various levels in six school systems in each of five states. In all of these, the states have instituted writing assessments in order to mandate the teaching of writing. All of the assessments also mandate certain types of writing simply by including them on the assessment. This amounts to the imposition of a new writing curriculum.

When teachers tell us about how they teach, they also frequently tell us how they feel about their students' abilities to succeed on the tests. The data analyzed so far indicate a pattern similar to the findings in this study. If their talk indicates an objectivist stance, and if they are not optimistic about their students, they also simplify what they teach through reduction and use a skill-and-drill methodology to teach the "how to" compositions or the five-paragraph theme, even though the tests do not require a five-paragraph theme.

I suspect that there is greater hope for teachers who are objectivist but also optimistic about their students' capabilities. Here at least is the possibility for surprise when students do not react well. Among these teachers we see more evidence of reflective practice in both planning and teaching. And as we have seen, many of them use some activities that allow the monitoring of student responses, for example, Professor Thomas's group discussion of student writing. Further, because these teachers occasionally exhibit a constructivist stance, there is greater chance for change.

If teacher knowledge is constructed as I have argued it is, and if epistemological stance plays an important role in its construction and use, then it is unlikely that teachers will change as a result of outside efforts to change methods or curriculum. Further, if epistemological stance and teacher knowledge have a powerful influence on reflective practice, direct efforts to help teachers become more reflective will very likely fail. Change in thinking and reflective practice will almost necessarily entail that teachers reconstruct their knowledge, especially if the teachers hold nonoptimistic beliefs about students and if they have adopted an objectivist epistemological stance. Reformers will have to find ways and means of helping teachers reconstruct their knowledge and stance.

One possibility lies in helping teachers to develop professional networks in which they can discuss their work with one another, become teacher researchers, and write about their thinking. Cochran-Smith and Lytle (1993) and Freedman (forthcoming) indicate the kinds of changes that such networks bring about. In a personal communication to me, Lytle indicated that such networks are very time (and energy)–consuming. But the rewards are potentially very great over periods of a year or two. However, membership in such networks is never mandatory.

Another possibility for instigating change is a model, which I will call a workshop, that has been in use with University of Chicago preservice teachers for over 25 years. The workshop involves four to five teachers in the planning, teaching, and evaluation of teaching in a single class. This is not the usual team teaching, in which the teaching tasks are divided in order to reduce the workload for each teacher. Rather, it is collaborative teaching in which all teachers participate in planning and evaluating each day's activities over a period of four to five weeks. Only one teacher teaches in a given class hour, but over the course of several weeks, all teachers participate equally in the teaching. In this model, someone must have detailed knowledge of how to invent the kinds of activities that engage students in learning and how to operate those activities in class. This person (one of the teachers, a consultant, or some other knowledgeable person) is crucial to the success of the teaching workshop. Without such a person, and probably other sources of knowledge, participants are likely to try only what they know and feel safe with. A more knowledgeable person can push the planning up a notch, provide suggestions as it progresses, guide evaluation of the teaching, and help participants gain insight into classroom events.

When the group deals with procedures that are new to them, they, in Schön's (1987) words, "deal often with uncertainty, uniqueness, and conflict. The non-routine situations of practice are at least partly indeterminate and must somehow be made coherent" (p. 157). To do that, Schön argues, they "frame" the "messy" problem by attending selectively to certain features, organize them, and set "a direction for action" (p. 4), which becomes a "frame experiment." Between the body of knowledge and theory available in a field and its skillful application in a concrete situation, Schön continues, there is always a "gap of knowledge." Bridging that gap requires "a thoughtful invention of new trials based on appreciation of the results of earlier moves. The application of such a rule to a concrete case must be mediated by an art of reflection-in-action" (p. 158). That is, the participants must engage in reflective practices. They learn to "conduct frame experiments in which they impose a kind of coherence on messy situations and thereby discover consequences and implications of their chosen frames" (p. 157). For Schön, the frame experiment is the essence of reflective practice and, I argue, the basis of inquiry in teaching.

We may think of one lesson's frame experiment as having five fluid features: (1) analyzing current student progress in relation to general course goals, for example, as related to writing; (2) positing some change or range of possible changes sought in the writing of students; (3) selecting or inventing a teaching strategy or set of strategies to implement the desired change, for example, procedures for a certain kind of writing task; (4) devising a plan for implementing the teaching strategies; (5) assessing the impact of the teaching strategy in order to "discover consequences and implications of [the] chosen frames" and evaluating the strategies themselves.

All workshop participants engage in planning such frame experiments every day as they plan the upcoming lesson. One person teaches. Those who are not teaching observe the class carefully. Their notes provide a host of information for follow-up discussions. Questions often begin with the extent to which the teaching achieved the results that the group was hoping for. The group examines what students wrote, and then proceeds to examine everything else, from seating arrangements that did not work well to conceptual problems with the lesson. After even a few days, the input of the skilled observer becomes less important, and the student teachers begin to take the lead in the collaborative reflection.

One study comparing student teachers who had been in such a workshop with others who had not found that the workshop people were far more likely to engage their classes in what I have called procedural knowledge, to use small group activities, to engage their students in discussion (rather than recitation), to use more authentic assessment, to engage their students in higher levels of discourse processing, and to reveal more reflective thinking about their own teaching (Johannessen, 1997). I am convinced that student teachers who have had this sort of experience continue to be far more reflective as teachers than those who have not.

Whether or not similar results would be possible with experienced teachers remains to be seen. However, I am convinced that some model such as this or the teacher-as-researcher model will have to be implemented if we are to see change across a given faculty.

IMPLICATIONS FOR RESEARCH

The model developed over the last several chapters depends heavily on both teacher statements about their practice and observations of their practice. Much of the existing research on teacher thinking relies primarily on analyses of teacher statements about their practice. Without my close attention to the observational data, in this study I would have missed the importance of knowledge of students and its impact on practice. Although teachers' talk comes close to revealing that their nonoptimistic attitudes lead to the simplification that we observed, the observational data provides strong support for the inferences involved and their confirmation. One clear implication of this research is that research on teacher thinking must involve observation of what teachers do in classrooms.

The observations also allow for definition of teacher concepts. For example, several teachers talk about discussion in their classrooms, but the observational data indicate that no real discussion takes place. By discussion, some of these teachers refer to their own talk as their students listen. Others refer to recitation. In addition, the observations allow for insight into knowledge in performance (Ryle, 1984).

Contrary to much of present research on teacher thinking, this study indicates that teacher thinking appears to be represented in argument form. This is not to say that knowledge is not represented in story form, but that decisions about practice clearly involve practical theories that take the form of arguments, not the paradigmatic form represented by Bruner (1985) in his advocacy of narrative, but in the kind of simple, everyday argument represented by Toulmin (1958). A second implication for research is that we need to recognize that not all thinking is either paradigmatic or narrative as Bruner suggests, but that much of it involves arguments in the form of claims, grounds, warrants (that may be no more than general definitions), backing, and rebuttal (Toulmin, 1958).

We have much still to learn about the nature of teacher thinking, about the specific roles of pedagogical content knowledge in the invention activities and in response to students, about the construction of curricula, and so forth. Most important of all, it seems to me, will be the research that provides greater insight into how teachers become reflective about their own practice. That knowledge will help us learn what must be done in the effective education of teachers.

References

Aristotle. (1947). *Metaphysics* (W. D. Ross, Trans.). In R. McKeon (Ed.), *Introduction to Aristotle*. New York: Random House.

Atran, S. (1990). *Cognitive foundations of natural history: Towards an anthropology of science*. New York: Cambridge University Press.

Axelrod, R. B., & Cooper, C. R. (1991). *The St. Martin's guide to writing*. New York: St. Martin's Press.

Bakhtin, M. (1981). *The dialogic imagination*. Austin: University of Texas Press.

Bazerman, C. (1988). *Shaping written knowledge: The genre and activity of the experimental article in science*. Madison: University of Wisconsin Press.

Bereiter, C., & Scardamalia, M. (1987). *The psychology of written composition*. Hillsdale, NJ: Erlbaum.

Berlin, J. A. (1982, December). Contemporary composition: The major pedagogical theories. *College English, 44*(8), 765–777.

Berlin, J. A. (1984). *Writing instruction in nineteenth-century American colleges*. Carbondale: Southern Illinois University Press.

Bloom, B. S., (Ed.) (1956). *Taxonomy of educational objectives: Cognitive domain*. New York: David Mckay.

Britton, J. N., Burgess, T., Martin, N., McLeod, A., & Rose, H. (1975). *The development of writing abilities (11–18)*. London: Macmillan.

Bruner, J. (1985). Narrative and paradigmatic modes of thought. In *Learning and teaching the ways of knowing* (84th Yearbook of the National Society for the Study of Education, Part 2) (pp. 97–115). Chicago: National Society for the Study of Education.

Clandinin, J. A. (1986). *Classroom practice: Teacher images in action*. London: Falmer Press.

Clandinin, D. J., & Connelly, F. M. (1995). *Teachers' professional knowledge landscapes*. New York: Teachers College Press.

Clark, C. M., & Peterson, P. L. (1986). Teachers' thought processes. In M. C. Wittrock (Ed.), *Handbook of research on teaching* (3rd edition, pp. 255–296). New York: Macmillan.

Cochran-Smith, M., & Lytle, S. L. (1993). *Inside/outside: Teacher research and knowledge*. New York: Teachers College Press.

Connelly, F. M., & Clandinin, D. J. (1988). *Teachers as curriculum planners: Narrative of experience*. New York: Teachers College Press.

Connors, R. J. (1981, December). The rise and fall of the modes of discourse. *College Composition and Communication, 32*(4), 444–455.

Cuban, L. (1988). A fundamental puzzle of school reform. *Phi Delta Kappan, 69*, 341–344.

Darling-Hammond, L., with Ancess, J. & Falk, B. (1995). *Authentic assessment in action: Studies of schools and students at work.* New York: Teachers College Press.

Elbaz, F. (1983). *Teacher thinking: A study of practical knowledge.* New York: Nichols.

Elbaz, F. (1991). Research on teachers' knowledge: The evolution of a discourse. *Journal of Curriculum Studies, 23*(1), 1–19.

Emig, J. (1971). *The composing process of twelfth graders.* Urbana, IL: National Council of Teachers of English.

Fenstermacher, G. D. (1994). The knower and the known: The nature of knowledge in research on teaching. *Review of Research in Education, 20,* 3–56.

Freedman, S. (forthcoming). *Literacy and learning: Teachers' research in the multicultural classroom.* New York: Teachers College Press.

Gadamer, H. G. (1976). D. E. Linge, trans. *Philosophical hermeneutics.* Berkeley and Los Angeles: University of California Press.

Goodlad, J. (1984). *A place called school: Prospects for the future.* New York: McGraw-Hill.

Grossman, P. L. (1990). *The making of a teacher: Teacher knowledge and teacher education.* New York: Teachers College Press.

Hartwell, P. (1985, February). Grammar, grammars, and the teaching of grammar. *College English, 47*(2), 105–127.

Hillocks, G., Jr. (1982, October). The interaction of instruction, teacher comment, and revision in teaching the composing process. *Research in the Teaching of English, 16*(3), 261–278.

Hillocks, G., Jr. (1986). *Research on written composition: New directions for teaching.* Urbana, IL: National Conference on Research in English/ERIC Clearinghouse on Reading and Communication Skills.

Hillocks, G., Jr. (1995). *Teaching writing as reflective practice.* New York: Teachers College Press.

Hillocks, G., & Smith, M. W. (1991). In J. Flood, J. M. Jensen, D. Lapp, & J. R. Squire (Eds.), *Handbook of research on teaching the English language arts.* New York: Macmillan.

Hirsch, E. D. (1982). Some principles of composition from grade school to grad school. In G. Hillocks (Ed.), *The English curriculum under fire: What are the real basics?* (pp. 39–52). Urbana, IL: National Council of Teachers of English.

Hoetker, J., & Ahlbrand, W. P., Jr. (1969). The persistence of the recitation. *American Educational Research Journal, 6,* 145–167.

Johannessen, L. R. (1997). *Examining pedagogical content knowledge in student teachers: A study of six student teachers from two graduate English education programs.* Unpublished doctoral dissertation.

Johannessen, L. R., Kahn, E. A., & Walter, C. C. (1982). *Designing and sequencing prewriting activities.* Urbana, IL: National Council of Teachers of English and ERIC Clearinghouse on Reading and Communication Skills.

Kahn, E. A. (1994). Assessing learning or controlling behavior? A case study of testing in a tenth-grade English course. University of Chicago: Unpublished paper.

Kahn, E. A., Johannessen, L. R., & Walter, C. C. (1984). *Writing about literature*. Urbana, IL: National Council of Teachers of English and ERIC Clearinghouse on Reading and Communication Skills.

Kinneavy, J. L. (1971). *A theory of discourse*. Englewood Cliffs, NJ: Prentice-Hall.

Kohler, W. (1959). *Gestalt psychology*. New York: New American Library.

Lee, C. D. (1993). *Signifying as a scaffold for literary interpretation: The pedagogical implications of an African American discourse genre* (NCTE Research Report No. 26). Urbana, IL: National Council of Teachers of English.

Lortie, D. (1975). *Schoolteacher*. Chicago: University of Chicago Press.

McEwan, H., & Bull, B. (1991, Summer). The pedagogic nature of subject matter knowledge. *American Educational Research Journal, 282*(2), 316–334.

McNeil, L. M. (1986). *Contradictions of control: School structure and school knowledge*. New York: Routledge.

Murray, L. (1849). *English grammar*. New York: Raynor.

North, S. (1987). *The making of knowledge in composition: Portrait of an emerging field*. Portsmouth, NH: Heinemann.

Nystrand, M., with Gamoran, A., Kachur, R., & Prendergast, C. (1997). *Opening dialogue: Understanding the dynamics of language and learning in the English classroom*. New York: Teachers College Press.

Ryle, G. (1984). *The concept of mind*. Chicago: University of Chicago Press.

Schön, D. A. (1987). *Educating the reflective practitioner: Toward a new design for teaching and learning in the professions*. San Francisco: Jossey-Bass.

Schultz, J. (1982). *Writing from start to finish: The "story workshop" basic forms rhetoric-reader*. Montclair, NJ: Boynton/Cook.

Shulman, L. S. (1986, March). Those who understand: Knowledge growth in teaching. *Educational Researcher, 15*(2), 4–14.

Shulman, L. S. (1987). Knowledge and teaching: Foundations of the new reform. *Harvard Educational Review, 57*(1), 1–22.

Smagorinsky, P., & Coppock, J. (1994, July). Cultural tools and the classroom context: An exploration of an artistic response to literature. *Written Communication, 11*(3), 283–310.

Stern, D. (1995). *Teaching English so it matters: Developing curricula for and with high school students*. Newberry Park, CA: Corwin Press.

Toulmin, S. (1958). *The uses of argument*. Cambridge, England: Cambridge University Press.

Troyka, L. Q. (1973). *A study of the effects of simulation-gaming on expository prose competence of remedial English composition students*. Unpublished doctoral dissertation, New York University.

Wilhelm, J. D. (1997). *"You gotta be the book": Teaching engaged and reflective reading with adolescents*. New York: Teachers College Press.

Index

AA (almost exclusively African American), 47, 54, 78

Ahlbrand, W.P., 134

"Apprenticeship of observation" (Lortie), 112

Argument, in teacher thinking, 72, 124, 137. *See also* Writing assignments

Aristotle, 1, 110

Assessment, 9, 18, 30, 34, 36, 42, 55–56, 64–69, 101
  authentic (Darling-Hammond), 42, 73
  state-mandated writing, 52, 71, 107, 134

Atran, S., 113

Authentic Assessment in Action (Darling-Hammond et al.), 42, 73

Axelrod, R.B., 71, 117

Bakhtin, Mikhail, 27

Ballard, Prof., 124

Basics, the, 120, 125

Bazerman, C., 72

Bede, The Venerable, 42

"Beer Street" (Hogarth), 14 (ill.), 11–18, 25, 112, 114, 118, 123, 129, 131–132

Bereiter, Carl, 66, 119

Berlin, James A., 57, 63, 71, 110–112, 118

Bloom, Benjamin, 61, 74

Britton, James, 29

Bruner, Jerome, 124, 137

Bull, B., 121–123, 127

Burke, Kenneth, 110

Cassirer, Ernst, 110

Changes in teaching, possibilities for, 21, 124–126, 134–137

Clandinin, D.J., 1–5, 124

Clark, C.M., 128

Classroom Practice (Clandinin), 2–3

Coaching, 31, 66–69, 79–80, 82, 88–92, 115, 118

Cochran-Smith, M, 135

Co-constructing knowledge, 86, 92–93, 112, 114, 117–118, 131, 135–136

Cognitive Foundations of Natural History (Atran), 113

Composing Process of Twelfth Graders (Emig), 73

Concept of Mind, The (Ryle), 23–24, 27, 122, 137

Conferencing, 32, 34, 39, 48, 80, 101

Connelly, F.M., 1–5, 124

Connors, R.J., 57, 71

Constructivism, 19, 23, 42, 70–71, 75–93, 102, 109–110, 111–112, 115, 119–120, 131–137
  effects on student achievement, 134

Constructivist, 75–93, 110–119, 131–132, 135–137

Content knowledge, 6, 19–21, 71–72, 121–124, 127. *See also* Pedagogical content knowledge

Content of writing.. *See* Substantive knowledge

Context knowledge, 6, 131–132

Contradictions of Control (McNeil), 42

Cooper, C.R., 71, 117

Coppock, J., 42

Crane, Stephen, 100

Curriculum, 5, 22, 30, 53, 94–108, 115–120, 134
  assumptions behind curricular decisions, 106–112, 118–119
  building block, 50, 107, 116
  constructions of students and, 119–120
  macro-, 24–25, 30, 57, 61–64, 73, 79, 91–92, 96–97, 105–106, 109, 116

Curriculum (*continued*)
  micro-, 25–27, 30, 57, 63–64, 72, 94–97,
    105–106, 109, 116, 118, 120
  personal commitments and, 107–108
  teachers' construction of, 97, 105, 112,
    116–120
  varying methods of separation (task
    analysis) and, 106–107, 119–120
Curriculum knowledge, 6, 22, 24–25, 30, 94,
  105, 109, 116, 123–124, 129, 132, 135

Danziger, Prof., 31–34, 36, 105, 107, 111,
  116–117
Darling-Hammond, Linda, 42
Declarative knowledge (of *what*), 27–29, 35–
  36, 39–43, 50–53, 63–66, 75–79, 95,
  103, 106, 120, 122, 131
Deduction (method of "classical" rhetoric), 111
"Defensive" teaching, 42
*Designing and Sequencing Prewriting
  Activities* (Johannessen, Kahn, & Walter)
Development of Writing Abilities, The (Britton
  et al.), 29
Dewey, John, 110, 121–122, 127
Dialect, 96, 133
  right to (Conference on College Communi-
    cation and Composition), 61, 74
Dialectic (method of "new" or "epistemic"
  rhetoric), 112, 115, 118
Dialogic Imagination, The (Bakhtin), 27
Dictation, 1, 97–100, 119
Direct instructions 6, 49
Discourse knowledge, 18, 21, 29, 34, 53–64,
  75–78, 103–106, 113, 119
Discussion, monologic (Nystrand), 9, 25–26,
  39, 41, 58, 76–77, 132
Discussion, small group, 11–15, 30, 32, 39,
  41–42, 48, 112, 114–115, 118, 120, 122,
  126, 128, 131
Discussion, teacher led, dialogic, 10–11, 16–
  17, 26–27, 30, 32, 39, 41–42, 66–70, 77,
  82–83, 85–86, 114–115, 129, 132, 135
Dobbs, Prof., 95–109, 114, 116–120, 124–125
Dynamics of teacher knowledge, 72–74, 109–
  125

Educating the Reflective Practitioner (Schön),
  2, 127–129, 136
Elbaz, F., 2–3, 5, 124
Emig, Janet, 73
English 98 (course number), 45–48, 97, 101–
  104, 119

English 100, 1, 44–48, 80–92, 95–102, 119
English 101, 44–48, 54–65, 98, 100, 119
English Grammar (Murray), 19
English Journal, 69
English, standard, 61
Enthymemes, 111
Environment, learning ("transformation of the
  world in which students act") (McEwan
  and Bull), 122–123
Episodes, teaching, 30–36, 76, 116
  assessment, 34, 48
  boundaries of, 32–33
  classification of knowledge in, 34–36
  discourse-centered, 77
  diversionary, 34–35, 48
  function of, 33–34
  identification of, 30–31
  instructional, 32–33, 38, 48, 79
  management, 34, 48
  substantive, 35, 38, 77, 79
Epistemology, 4–6, 18–21, 109–112, 115–
  120, 124–129, 131, 134–137
Evaluation of consequences (reflective), 123,
  128–130, 136
*Examining Pedagogical Content Knowledge
  in Student Teachers* (Johannessen), 136
Exercises, 95–99, 102, 113–114, 129, 134
Explanation of procedures (giving directions),
  36, 50–51, 75
Exposition.. *See* Writing assignments
Expressivist rhetoric. Rhetoric

Farewell to Arms, A (Hemingway), 97–99
Feedback, 53, 65–69, 112
Fenstermacher, G.D., 2, 127
Five-paragraph theme. *See* Writing assignments
Formal-rhetorical knowledge, 34, 39–41,
  49–51, 53–64, 70, 73, 75–76, 95,
  103–104, 106, 111–113
*Forms of Intellectual and Ethical
  Development in the College Years, The*
  (Perry), 123, 151
Fragmented instruction, 106–107, 119–120
Frame experiments (Schön), 128–129, 136
Freedman, S., 135
Frontal instruction (Goodlad), 32, 39, 41, 43,
  48–49, 63, 67, 77

Gadamer, Hans Georg, 19
Genre, 53
Gestalt Psychology (Kohler), 19
"Ghost in the Machine" (Ryle), 23

Gilray, John, 10–11, 26, 107, 114
"Gin Lane" (Hogarth), 13 (ill.), 11–18, 25,
    112, 114, 118, 123, 129, 131–132
Goals. *See* Purposes (in teaching)
Goodlad, John, 25, 32, 39, 70, 134
Gow, Mr., 10–19, 25–29, 34–35, 39, 41, 51,
    64, 70, 77, 79, 90, 93, 105–124, 128–134
Grammar. *See* Writing, parts of
Green, Prof., 79–95, 105–124, 128, 131,
Grossman, Pamela, 2, 20–24, 69, 94, 105, 116

Hartwell, P., 23
Hemingway, Ernest, 97, 99
High school English, 9–19, 25–29, 50, 71,
    105–107, 121
Hillocks, George, Jr., 39, 72, 76, 113, 117, 134
Hirsch, E.D., 96
Hoetker, J., 134
Hogarth, William, 13–14 (ills.), 11–18, 25,
    112, 114, 118, 123, 129, 131–132

Imitation (in instruction), 99–100
Independent seat work, 9, 32, 39, 48, 129
Individualized instruction, 102
Induction (method of "current traditional
    rhetoric"), 111
Inquiry (investigating content), 76, 112, 115
Inside/Outside (Cochran Smith & Lytle), 135
Instruction, time spent on, 38, 41, 48–49
Introductory activities, 10–11, 25, 81, 107,
    114
Instrumental purposes, 69–74, 94, 97. *See
    also* Purposes (in teaching)
Invention, by teachers, 122–125, 135–137.
    See also Curriculum, teachers'
    construction of

James, Prof., 36, 40, 60–64, 70, 73–75, 94,
    105, 109, 111, 113, 116–117, 120, 124–
    125, 129
Jenkins, Prof., 76–77
Johannessen, L.R., 122, 136
Julius Caesar (Shakespeare), 105

Kahn, E.A., 42, 122
Kazan, Elia, 81
Kinneavy, James L., 71
Knowledge
    dynamics of teacher's, 72–74, 109–125
    impact of teacher's, 22, 105–108, 117–125,
        135–137
    of learning processes, 94, 106–109, 121–124

in performance (Ryle), 23–24, 122, 137
of students, 6, 19, 21–22, 30, 43–48, 53–69,
    72, 94, 109, 119–124, 128–129, 131,
    135–137
teacher's personal, 1–5, 124: images, 3,
    128; metaphor, 3, 5; narrative, 3–5,
    124, 137; rhythm, 3; rules, 3, 23, 109,
    131
Kohler, W., 19
Kramer, Prof., 101–104, 106, 109, 112–113,
    117, 119, 124, 128, 130–133

Langer, Susanne, 110
Learning
    as acts of construction, 81, 92, 112
    as amalgam of construction and repetition,
        102–103, 112
    formal theories of, 123
    as mechanical repetition, 95–96, 113
    "overlearning" (Prof. Dobbs), 95–96, 113
    practical theories of, 113–117, 124
Lector, Mr., 25–27, 29, 34
Lecture (as form of instruction), 5, 7–8, 19,
    32, 35, 42, 53, 60, 66, 70, 75, 79, 99–
    100, 103–104, 109, 112–114, 117, 126,
    129, 134
Lee, C.D., 122
Literacy and Learning (Freedman), 135
logic, 111
Lortie, Dan, 112, 124
Lytle, S.L., 135

Making of Knowledge in Composition, The
    (North), 113
Making of a Teacher, The (Grossman), 2, 20,
    22, 24, 69, 94, 105, 116
Management activities, 33–34, 48
McEwan, H., 121–123, 127
McNeil, L.M., 42
Mechanical correctness, 1, 8, 35, 61, 75, 95–
    104, 112–114, 129–131
Mechanical-syntactical knowledge, 34, 39–41,
    49–53, 75–76, 96–104, 117. *See also*
    Writing assignments
Metaphysics (Aristotle), 1
Mind/matter distinction (Ryle), 23
"Modest Proposal, A" (Swift), 61, 125
Modeling (by teacher), 1, 46, 57–58, 66, 76–
    77
Models, 8–9, 18, 33, 61, 80–81, 76–91, 99–
    100, 115–117, 129
Murray, Lindley, 19

Narrative. *See* Writing assignments
Nonoptimism (of teachers about students),
   43–44, 61, 72–73, 78, 119, 129, 132, 134
   abstract content and, 51, 56, 78
   course level and, 47–48
   distrust in students' independent thinking
      and, 43–44, 48–50, 53, 72, 93
   dogmatism and, 58–59, 96, 132–134
   ethnicity of students and, 46–48
   gender and, 46–47
   lecture and, 47–49, 99–100, 132–133
   perceptions of students' deficiencies and,
      43–44, 48–49, 54–55, 61, 73–74, 78,
      95, 132–134
   reductive, inauthentic "structuring" of
      activities and, 119, 132–133
   simplification of content and, 43–44, 53,
      56, 72, 74, 95, 106, 111, 119–120,
      132–134, 137
   simplification of purpose and, 69–71, 74,
      95–101, 125
   substantive facilitation (Bereiter and
      Scardamalia) and, 66, 101, 119
North, S., 113
Nystrand, Martin, 25–26, 39, 70, 134

Objectivism, 18–19, 42, 93, 102, 109, 112,
   114–115, 117–119, 121, 129–134
Opening Dialogue (Nystrand et al.), 25–26,
   39, 70, 134
Optimism (of teachers about students), 43, 72,
   79, 86, 92, 129–132, 135
   allowances for special circumstances and,
      43, 45–46, 132
   allowing freedom and responsibility and,
      43, 45–46, 48–50
   authentic assessment and, 73, 132
   constructed upon students' responsiveness
      to offered instruction, 119, 129, 132
   constructivist epistemology and, 132
   course level and, 47–48
   encouragement of creative thinking and,
      45–46, 70, 74, 80–91
   engagement of student interest and, 102–
      103, 120, 131
   ethnicity of students and, 47, 79
   finding validity in alternative viewpoints
      and, 62, 74
   gender and, 46–47
   individualized instruction and, 102
   intervention and, 128–129, 132, 135–136
   liking for students and, 45, 86

procedural facilitation (Bereiter and
      Scardamalia) and, 66–69, 120
   procedural knowledge and, 50–51, 73–74,
      79–93
   progressive complexity of curriculum and,
      61–63, 73, 106–107, 120, 132
   revision of unsuccessful lessons and, 61,
      125, 128–129, 136
   student-centered activities and, 132
   time on instruction and, 48
Outlining, 8–9, 18, 45

Paradigmatic knowledge (Bruner), 137
Paragraph. *See* Writing, parts of
Perry, William, 62, 74
Pedagogical content knowledge (Shulman), 6,
   18, 20–22, 24–25, 30, 94, 109, 120–124,
   135–137
Pessimism. *See* Nonoptimism
Peterson, P.L., 128
Philosophical Hermeneutics (Gadamer), 19
Place Called School, A (Goodlad), 25, 32, 39,
   70, 134
Practical knowledge, 2–5, 23–24, 94, 123–124
Practical theories in teacher thinking, 113–
   114, 129, 131, 137
Presentational (vs. representational)
   instruction, 63, 78, 122, 129, 133. *See
   also* Frontal instruction; Discussion,
   monologic (Nystrand)
Procedural facilitation (Bereiter and
   Scardmalia), 66–69, 120
Procedural knowledge (*how*), 27–29, 33–36,
   39–42, 48–53, 60, 64, 75, 78–93, 95,
   106, 111–112, 136
Psychology Today (magazine), 95
Psychology of Written Composition (Bereiter
   and Scardamalia), 66, 119
Punctuation. *See* Writing, parts of
Purpose (in writing), 75–76
Purposes (in teaching), 54, 56, 61–62, 69–74
   teachers' knowledge of, 6, 21–22, 30, 54,
      56, 61–62, 68–74, 109, 115–120, 123–
      124, 129, 131
PW (predominantly white), 47, 95

Reading level, writing ability and, 101
Realism, Scottish common sense, 57, 110
Recalling images, 80–86, 107, 111, 114–115,
   118
Recitation, 39, 70, 75, 113, 117, 126, 129,
   132, 134

Reconstruction, 70–72, 111, 114–115
Reduction (to inauthentic tasks), 119, 132–134
Reflective practice (Schön), 2, 20–22, 124, 126–137
REM (racially and ethnically mixed), 47, 60, 79
Research, contrasted with reflective practice, 127–128
Research methodologies for determining teacher knowledge and its impact on practice, 126, 137
  classroom observation, 2, 4, 7–20, 22–25, 29–36, 43, 48–49, 63, 65–69, 76–78, 80–89, 99–100, 103–104, 137
  curricular analysis, 5–6, 20, 24–27, 61–63, 71–74, 79, 96–101, 103–108, 135–137
  discourse analysis (interviews), 2, 4, 22, 24, 30, 43–48, 54–62, 79–81, 90–91, 95–101, 104, 137
  epistemological analysis, 5–6, 109–112. See also Constructivism, Objectivism
  teacher research, 135, 137
Research on Written Composition (Hillocks), 39, 76, 117, 134
Research, types of instruction, 60
Rhetoric, 29, 34, 39–41, 49–51, 60, 71–72, 109–112, 115–116, 118
  classical (Berlin), 110–111. See also Deduction
  current traditional (Berlin), 57, 63–64, 71–72, 110–112, 116. See also Induction
  expressivist, 110–111, 117–118
  new or epistemic (Berlin), 110–112, 118–119. See also Dialectic
Rose, Prof., 54–60, 63–66, 70, 73–78, 103, 105, 110–120, 125
Richards, I.A., 110
Ryle, Gilbert, 23–24, 27, 122, 137

St. Martin's Guide to Writing (Axelrod and Cooper), 71, 117
Scardamalia, M., 66, 119
Scholarship
  contrasted with pedagogy, 122–123, 127
  and the development of hypotheses, 127
  pedagogical assumptions of, 121–122
Schön, Donald, 3, 127–129, 136
Schoolteacher (Lortie), 112, 124
Schulz, J., 79
Separation of learning tasks, 106–107
Shakespeare, William, 76–77, 105
Shaping Written Knowledge (Bazerman), 72
Shulman, Lee, 2, 5–6, 20, 69, 94, 121, 123

Signifying as a Scaffold for Literary Interpretation (Lee), 122
Smagorinsky, Peter, 42
Smith, Michael W., 113
Spelling. See Writing, parts of
Standard English, 61, 74, 95–96, 130–131
Standards, performance, 24, 134
Stern, Deborah, 122
Strategic instruction (manipulation of substance), 10–19, 79–80, 83, 85–91, 106, 110–114, 120
Student-centered activities, 5, 10–19, 25–29, 42, 64, 70, 76–93, 106, 110, 112, 115–124, 131, 134–137
Study of the Effects of Simulation-Gaming on Expository Prose Competence of Remedial English Composition Students (Troyka), 122
Subject matter, 6, 21–24, 34, 94, 127. See also Curriculum; Knowledge, types of
Substantive facilitation (Bereiter and Scardamalia), 66, 101, 119
Substantive knowledge (potential content), 21, 29, 34, 39–41, 49–53, 56–60, 63–69, 75–93, 95, 103, 112–113
Swift, Jonathan, 61
Syllogisms, 111

Task analysis. See Knowledge, types of teacher
Taxonomy of Educational Objectives (Bloom), 61, 74
Teacher education, 126, 134–137
  for positive expectations and constructivist epistemological stances, 135–136
Teacher lore (North), 113
Teacher Thinking (Elbaz), 2–3
Teachers as Curriculum Planners (Connelly and Clandinin), 1–5
Teachers' Professional Knowledge Landscapes (Clandinin and Connelly), 2, 124
Teaching English So It Matters (Stern), 122
Teaching Writing as Reflective Practice (Hillocks), 72
Technical rationality (opposed to reflective practice), 127–128
Text, programmed, 79–80
Textbooks, 71–72, 79–80, 96, 105, 111–112, 124, 132
Textual explication, 10–19, 25–29, 76–77, 81, 85–86

Theory, behind practice (Aristotle), 2, 109–
    113, 134–137
Thomas, Prof., 66–70, 74–77, 93, 109, 117,
    122, 135
Thought/action distinction (Ryle), 23–27,
    122, 137
Toulmin, S.E., 72, 137
Troyka, L.Q., 122
Truth, 110–112
Tutoring, 104

Uses of Argument, The (Toulmin), 72, 137

Vocabulary. See Writing, parts of
"Voluptuary Under the Horrors of Digestion,
    A" (Gilray), 10–11, 26, 107, 114

Wade, Prof., 7–10, 18–19, 76, 109
Walker in the City, A (Kazan), 81
Walter, C. C., 122
Warriner's high school composition textbooks
    (Harcourt Brace), 71
Wilhelm, J.D., 69
Wooden, John, 95
Worksheets, 104, 112
Workshop, 79,92
Writing About Literature (Kahn, Johannessen,
    and Walter), 122
Writing assignments
    analogy, 57
    argument (persuasion, evaluation), 18, 57,
        61–64, 71–72, 78–79, 105, 111–115,
        118–120, 129, 132
    cause and effect, 56, 71, 105, 111, 116
    classification, 8–9, 45, 54, 57–59, 63–64,
        71, 75, 105, 111, 113, 116
    comparison-contrast, 71, 111, 113, 116
    copying text, 97
    definition, 57, 71, 113, 116
    description, 31, 54, 56, 79, 116–117
    dictation, 1, 97–99
    examples, 71–72, 111
    exposition, 57–59, 61–62, 64, 71–72, 79,
        105, 111–112, 116, 118
    expressive, 71, 80–92, 110
    five-paragraph theme, 42, 51–52, 55–56,
        59, 64, 73, 75, 113, 116–117, 119–
        120, 133–134
    interpretation, 10–18, 27–28, 42, 106, 110,
        112, 115–116, 118, 123, 132

literary criticism, 116
mechanics, usage, and syntax, 29, 44–45, 49,
    73, 95–101, 105, 109, 116, 119, 129–
    131
narrative, 1, 35, 54–56, 59–60, 64, 71, 79–91,
    95, 100–101, 105–107, 111, 116–119
problem and solution, 61, 63
research, 60, 73, 106
single paragraph, 50, 71, 107, 133
Writing from Start to Finish (Schultz), 79
Writing Instruction in Nineteenth-Century
    American Colleges (Berlin), 57, 63, 71,
    110–112, 118
Writing, parts of
    body, 51, 72
    conclusion, 59, 72
    criteria, 63–64
    details, 59, 63, 79
    dialogue, 100, 106–107, 113–114
    examples, 57–59, 64
    grammar, 23, 31, 45, 96, 101, 107, 116,
        129–131
    imagery, 89, 110, 112, 114–117
    introduction, 52, 59, 72
    paragraph, 52, 103–107, 113, 119–120, 133
    punctuation, 96–100, 106–107, 114, 119
    sentence, 31, 96, 105, 107, 116
    thesis statement, 52, 67, 72
    topic sentence, 68
Writing, process of, 34, 104, 117
    brainstorming, 57, 76, 103, 112, 120, 122
    drafting (writing), 32, 80
    editing, 32–34, 54, 103, 120
    free writing, 80
    peer feedback, 117
    prewriting, 32, 80, 117
    revising, 32, 66–68, 80, 91–93, 103, 117
Writing, qualities of
    audience awareness, 53–55, 60–62, 73, 75
    conformity to conventions (mechanical
        correctness), 34, 40, 49, 95–107, 111,
        113, 116, 119
    feeling (receptivity, empathy), 91–92, 111,
        114–115
    purpose, 53, 75
    substance, 75, 105–106
    vision, 111, 115
    voice, 86, 91, 110–111, 115, 117
Writing, research in the teaching of, 76, 122,
    136–137

About the Author

GEORGE HILLOCKS, JR., received his B.A. in English from the College of Wooster, a Diploma in English Studies from the University of Edinburgh (Scotland), and his M.A. and Ph.D. from Case Western Reserve University. He taught secondary school English in Euclid, Ohio, where he was Director of the Project English Demonstration Center from 1963 to 1965. He taught English at Bowling Green State University where he served as Director of Freshman English Programs. Since 1971 he has been at the University of Chicago where he is currently professor in the Department of Education and the Department of English Language and Literature and continues to serve as Director of the Master of Arts in Teaching/English and as advisor to the graduate program in English Education. His articles have appeared in the *American Journal of Education, Research in the Teaching of English, American Educational Research Journal, English Journal, English Education, College English*, and other journals. He is author or coauthor of several books and monographs, including *Research on Written Composition: New Directions for Teaching*, published by the National Conference on Research in English. His most recent book is *Teaching Writing as Reflective Practice* published by Teachers College Press in 1995, which won NCTE's David H. Russell Award for Distinguished Research in the Teaching of English.